THE BIBLE AND THE BLACKBOARD

Biblical Solutions for Failing Schools

DR. GARY CASS

SAM KASTENSMIDT

ANTHONY URTI

THE BIBLE AND THE BLACKBOARD: Biblical Solutions for Failing Schools

Unless otherwise indicated, all Scripture quotations are from the New King James Version.

Cover design by Roark Creative: www.roarkcreative.com

Published by Coral Ridge Ministries
Printed in the United States of America

Coral Ridge Ministries
Post Office Box 1920
Fort Lauderdale, Florida 33302-1920
800-988-7884
letters@coralridge.org
www.coralridge.org

ISBN 978-1-929626-31-1

CONTENTS

INTRODUCTION
Dr. Gary Cass 5

THE BIBLE AND EDUCATION
Dr. Gary Cass 7

THE FOUNDERS AND EDUCATION
Sam Kastensmidt 17

FROM THE FOUNDERS TO DEWEY: THE ROLE OF IDEAS
Anthony Urti 27

MEASURING THE DECLINE
Sam Kastensmidt 39

MORAL COLLAPSE
Sam Kastensmidt 53

PARENTS VS. THE STATE
Sam Kastensmidt 65

ALTERNATIVES THAT WORK
Dr. Gary Cass and Sam Kastensmidt 75

ENDNOTES 87

INTRODUCTION

"Religion, morality, and knowledge, being necessary to good government and the happiness of mankind, schools and the means of education shall forever be encouraged."

THE NORTHWEST ORDINANCE OF 1787

"If the posted copies of the Ten Commandments are to have any effect at all, it will be to induce the school children to read, meditate upon, perhaps to venerate and obey, the Commandments.... [This] is not a permissible state objective."

U.S. SUPREME COURT, 1980

The education of children is the place where the culture war is engaged in its most critical struggle. It is the battle to shape the minds of the next generation, and thereby, the future of our nation.

We are told, however, that public education is a "neutral" realm, one where all ideas are given a free and fair hearing. Yet example after example reveals that Christian children are often told they cannot mention God or Jesus in classwork and other assignments.

There is a wealth of evidence to suggest that the public school system is overtly hostile to theism, in general, and Judeo-Christianity, in particular. Indeed, public schools have become a pseudo-secular church of humanism—not merely devoid of any mention of God, but also charged with animosity toward biblical truth. Consequently, public school teachers have been thrust into a new role—one in which they serve, willingly or not, as the clergy of this religion of secularism.

It is interesting to note that it was common and even expected in the early years of our nation for local ministers to preside over the education of the children in their communities. Ministers sat on school boards as a normal part of their vocation. Once I discovered this, my conscience, as a senior minister of a San Diego area church, began to bother me. Eventually, I ran for and was elected to the local high school board.

Things, as I discovered firsthand, have changed significantly since the nineteenth century, when clergy were welcomed to the governance of local schools. For some today, I found out, the mere thought of a theologically conservative, Bible-believing pastor on a school board was scandalous. Of course, a theologically liberal minister would be quite welcome.

This experience on the board was quite an eye opener. For example, during my six-year tenure, the board had to adopt textbooks for the District. The board had to select from a very narrow choice of state-approved text books that met state standards. Some texts were worse than others, but often in their attempt to be "neutral," the texts assumed the truth of both naturalism and Darwinism. Some were influenced heavily by Marxist economic and historical theories. In an apparent attempt not to offend, there was very little reference to the religious and spiritual motivations of some of the key persons and movements in our nation's history. Clearly this was not a "neutral" treatment.

Despite the war of values that rages within the public school arena, some Christians view education as a matter that is properly within the control of the state and outside the concern and jurisdiction of the Church. Yet according to apostolic preaching, Jesus Christ has been made "Lord of all."[1] What Christian could possibly argue that this all-encompassing lordship was meant to exclude the education of His little ones?

Christ's will regarding education is no mystery. On this or any other matter, Christians are responsible to proclaim "the whole counsel of God."[2] The modern Church cannot be faithful to Christ and remain silent on this most central front in the battle for the soul of America.

The Bible and the Blackboard aims to provide a clear understanding of the classic, relevant biblical passages on education. In addition, it will trace the evolution of the vastly different educational philosophies that have existed from America's founding to the modern day. Indeed, since the biblical and classical approach to education has been abandoned, academic standards have plummeted, common morality has collapsed, and parental rights have been utterly trampled. This book will diagnose the problems of public education, their sources, and offer commonsense solutions to help you as a parent and a citizen makes wise, biblical, and well-informed choices for your children.

Dr. Gary Cass
Executive Director
Center for Reclaiming America for Christ

THE BIBLE AND EDUCATION

"Whatever you do, do all to the glory of God."

I CORINTHIANS 10:31

DR. GARY CASS

It is almost universally accepted that the goal of education is to make good, productive (read "compliant and employable") citizens. That's it. For secular educators, the spiritual realm is either not real or, if real, not pertinent. The practical needs of society have taken the place of education that acknowledges God and recognizes the Bible as His revelation. Is this progress? You be the judge, in light of the troubled state of public education.

Certainly, education was not always seen as just a way to socialize Johnny and make him a willing and skilled worker.

Education, seen biblically, has a much loftier objective. Rightly conceived, the training of the mind is much more than a way of staying out of jail, off drugs, and out of the unemployment line. Education can indeed serve to glorify God and equip us to help our fellow man.

FAITH PRECEDES KNOWLEDGE

Education is, one would think, the pursuit of truth. In fact, one of Christ's most oft-quoted sayings is etched on the halls of prestigious universities around the world: "You shall know the truth, and the truth shall make you free."[1] Ripped from its context, it seems to assert that man can find truth on his own and that education can bring liberation. But that is not what Jesus said.

Jesus prefaced his oft-quoted saying with this admonition: "'If you abide in My word, you are My disciples indeed. And you shall know the truth, and the truth shall make you free.'"[2] Jesus was speaking to those who already believed in Him. He made knowledge of the truth dependent on abiding, or learning from, His word.

It is His words, not human reason on its own that are the source of liberating truth.

Jesus did not say abstract truth sets you free. *Faith in Jesus Christ sets you free.* You are proved to be His liberated people as you abide and grow in His liberating words. Thus, illuminating grace and spiritual regeneration by faith precede true learning.

The unbeliever's starting place for education is very different. Secular educational theorists reject God's revelation in Scripture—substituting it with finite, fallible, and autonomous human reasoning. The futility of this approach has been acknowledged from the outset of humanist philosophy. Even Plato, the pre-eminent non-Christian philosopher, admitted the same in his work, *Phaedo*, when he compared the search for ultimate truth on the basis of reason alone to "sailing in the seas of darkness on a small raft." Even so, the skeptics of our age still insist that human reason is the ultimate source of real knowledge.

Though non-believers, as creatures created in God's rational image, certainly make sound scientific discoveries about the particulars of this created world, the true meaning of their discoveries (as a window into the wisdom and glory of God in the face of Jesus Christ) is lost.

Christ declared, "For this cause I was born, and for this cause I have come into the world, that I should bear witness to the truth. Everyone who is of the truth hears My voice."[3] Those who reject Christ and His revelation in Scripture may enjoy some fruitfulness in this life, but are subject to futility in ultimate matters. As the Apostle Paul declared: "Where is the wise? Where is the scribe? Where is the disputer of this age? Has not God made foolish the wisdom of this world? ... Because the foolishness of God is wiser than men, and the weakness of God is stronger than men."[4]

LEARNING AS WORSHIP!

God has created man with rational abilities as a reflection of His own image. This fact of nature brings with it both the right and the duty to become good stewards of these faculties.

Jesus answered him, "The first of all the commandments is: 'Hear, O Israel, the LORD our God, the LORD is one. And you shall love the LORD your God with all your heart, with all your soul, **with all your mind**, and with all your strength.' This is the first commandment. And the second, like it, is this: 'You shall love your neighbor as yourself.' There is no other commandment greater than these."[5]

Loving God with all of our mind—by thinking His thoughts after Him, loving what He loves and affirming what He affirms—is every man's moral obligation. Education then has a very high, transcendent purpose. It is preparation for eternity! As Moses prayed in Psalm 90: "So teach us to number our days, that we may apply our hearts unto wisdom."[6]

Because humans are being shaped for an eternal destiny, we must be vigilant to oppose all thoughts that are contrary to Christ and His truth—"casting down imaginations, and every high thing that exalteth itself against the knowledge of God, and bringing into captivity every thought to the obedience of Christ."[7] In this world, thoughts can be divided between those that honor God and those that are idolatrous, that exalt man over God.

EDUCATION REQUIRES A RATIONAL BASIS

"Great is our lord and of great power;" declares Psalm 147, "his understanding is infinite!"[8]

The premises of secular thought—taken to their logical conclusion—undermine and, ultimately, destroy the very idea of education. Those who reject God contend that reality is simply matter plus time plus chance. If this is true, there is no possibility of true knowledge and thus, education. If we, like everything else in the universe, are merely chance combinations of atoms—without a soul—then reality is ultimately irrational because all things are the product of blind chance. But knowledge presupposes order and meaning; it cannot be a result of chance. If it is, irrationalism becomes ultimate.

Of course, no one lives as if they really believe that chance is the source of all things. Few secular educators, with the exception of those consistent secular materialists who deny rationality, would want to be accused of engaging in an irrational endeavor—but they are!

Christian education, by contrast, is based on the existence of a rational, living God. It is God, as theologian Charles Hodge has said, who makes knowledge possible: "What, therefore, we must hold fast to, if we would hold fast to God, is, that knowledge in God is knowledge… in its essential nature."[9]

The Scriptures are replete with verses that affirm God's exhaustive knowledge of all things.[10] The Apostle John wrote, "For God is greater than our hearts, and he knows *everything*."[11] Christianity affirms that reality reflects the unchanging nature of God. Thus, true scientific knowledge is possible because the nature of reality reflects the character of the Creator. Reality is rational because He is rational. Scientists, therefore, can with reason expect things to behave according to physical laws since God has written those laws into their very nature.

Today, the public schools and universities are filled with instructors who reject God and the notion of absolute truth—even the notion that anything can be known for certain. Ironically, these teachers spend their entire careers educating others that education is meaningless. The words of the Apostle Paul ring true: "Has not God made foolish the wisdom of this world?"[12]

The Christian has a much grander ideal. The human mind is to be employed and nurtured in fitting ways as an act of love to God.[13] Jesus came to mankind as the very "Logos," the Word of God,[14] "in whom are hidden *all* the treasures of wisdom and knowledge."[15] He can be comprehended by the renewed spiritual mind of man.[16] We can and should fashion our minds into an altar of worship to our triune God.[17]

THE UNIFYING PHILOSOPHY OF EDUCATION: THE TRIUNE GOD

If humanism leads to irrationality, where can mankind go to find a unifying philosophy of education? Don't look to modern higher education. The universities most certainly do not have a unified philosophy! If you attend classes at any secular institution, you will see that there is no unified coherent center around which the various departments of education coalesce—unless one considers chance coherent. No wonder there is such an emphasis on diversity at the university! This compartmentalization of the various departments of learning renders futile any attempt to make coherent sense of the whole of a person's life.

The most that modern education can muster are some disconnected facts and theories about particular subjects. They can say in a very limited way "what is" through scientific experiments—and perhaps even "how" some things work. However, modern education most certainly cannot explain "why" things are—apart from random chance.

If a philosophy of education cannot explain why mankind is here, then it cannot direct mankind as to where it should go. With no ultimate goal in sight beyond the grave, it has no grounds for asserting how or why things ought to be. Yet modern educators do not let that stop them. They hide behind the respectability of academia and make emphatic declarations about how things are and ought to be all the time.

Aleksandr Solzhenitsyn, the famous Russian author and historian, recognized the illogical nature of this worldview. "That which is called humanism—but what would be more correctly called irreligious anthropocentrism—cannot yield answers to the most essential questions of our life," he said.

If there is no God, then man becomes the final arbiter of truth. After all, in order to be certain that God does not exist, one would have to be all knowing and present everywhere for all eternity. Thus, in order to argue that there is no "higher being," an atheist must believe that he is the "highest being."

The arrogant assertions of humanism echo the old Greek cynic Protagoras, calling out from the grave: "Man is the measure of all things."[18] Or perhaps one can hear the tempting hissed whisper, "[I]n the day you eat of it your eyes will be opened, and you will be like God..."[19]

To the contrary, only the Christian worldview can make sense of the whole of life. Gordon Clark, the famed theologian, explained,

> There is only one metaphysics, one philosophy, that can really unify education and life. That philosophy is the philosophy of Christian theism; that metaphysics is the metaphysics of the being of the Triune God. What is needed is an educational system based on the Being of the Triune God.[20]

The Christian understands how there can be such a thing as a person with self-consciousness, volition, and emotions, because we are created by a personal, volitional, self-conscious God. Evolution's theory of origins turns human self-consciousness into nothing more than a fortuitous accident and no more valuable than a rock (another chance collection of molecules).

Christians can account for rational communication because God is rational and communicative. He revealed Himself through the prophets in Holy Scripture and most fully in the person of Christ, "the Word." So words and truth are definite. In a relativistic society, chance destroys communication, because our apprehension of words or truth may arbitrarily change at any moment. Thus, there is no truth, because what is true for you may be false for me.

Christianity teaches that Truth is the truth—no matter what anyone says. It exists independently from human apprehension; it is the very nature of the same God, [Christ] declared, "I am the way, the truth, and the life. No one comes to the Father except through Me." [21]

Christians can account for the reality of interpersonal relationships because God exists forever in a perfect union as Father, Son and Holy Spirit. Chance, however, renders our union with others, even our parents, spouses, and children, as insignificant irrational accidents and perhaps even illusions of random molecular brain activity. Yet even the most hardened cynic grieves at the loss of friends and family. He, too, is made in the image of God and knows, despite his protestations, that life and death are much more than just meaningless chance.

THE BEGINNING OF EDUCATION: REVERENCE FOR GOD

"The fear of the LORD is the beginning of wisdom." – Psalm 111:10

"No Fear" is emblazoned on the T-shirts of young people across America. America may be the "home of the brave," but this slogan is, in fact, a fitting symbol for a generation that has forgotten God.

This is nothing new. King David lamented that so many in his day had no fear of God.

> An oracle within my heart concerning the transgression of the wicked:
>
> There is no fear of God before his eyes. For he flatters himself in his own eyes, when he finds out his iniquity and when he hates. The words of his mouth are wickedness and deceit; he has ceased to be wise and to do good. He devises wickedness on his bed; he sets himself in a way that is not good; he does not abhor evil.[22]

Pride, hatred, deceit, wickedness, and a tolerance for evil—sound familiar? All are consequences of rejecting the fear of the Lord. Is it any wonder that public education is unable to stem the tidal wave of school violence, teen suicide, and an epidemic of sexual abuse with the hollow platitudes of humanism?

We learn in Proverbs that "The fear of the LORD is the beginning of wisdom."[23] To the ears of the modern skeptic, this proposal is like scratching fingernails across a blackboard. To those willing to travel an ancient, well-tested educational path, it is the way out of the despair and emptiness that humanism has been depositing into the minds of America's children for decades.

The classic Christian understanding of Proverbs 1:7 and the centrality of "the fear of the Lord" as the most essential Christian instructional goal is found in Puritan Matthew Henry's *Commentary*:

Of all things that are to be known, this is most evident, that God is to be feared, to be reverenced, served, and worshipped; this is so the beginning of knowledge that those know nothing who do not know this. As all our knowledge must take rise from the fear of God, so it must tend to it as its perfection and centre. Those know enough who know how to fear God, who are careful in every thing to please him and fearful of offending him in any thing; this is the Alpha and Omega of knowledge.[24]

THE WISDOM OF GOD

A quick survey of Proverbs, written for the instruction of the young, describes the "fear of the Lord" and its consequences for both life and learning:

- "Because they hated knowledge and did not choose the fear of the LORD, they would have none of my counsel and despised my every rebuke" (Proverbs 1:29-30).

- "The fear of the LORD is to hate evil; pride and arrogance and the evil way and the perverse mouth I hate" (Proverbs 8:13).

- "The fear of the LORD is the beginning of wisdom, and the knowledge of the Holy One is understanding. For by me your days will be multiplied, and years of life will be added to you" (Proverbs 9:10-11).

- "The fear of the LORD prolongs days, but the years of the wicked will be shortened" (Proverbs 10:27).

- "In the fear of the LORD there is strong confidence, and His children will have a place of refuge. The fear of the LORD is a fountain of life, to turn one away from the snares of death" (Proverbs 14:26-27).

- "Better is a little with the fear of the LORD, than great treasure with trouble" (Proverbs 15:16).
- "The fear of the LORD is the instruction of wisdom, and before honor is humility" (Proverbs 15:33).
- "In mercy and truth Atonement is provided for iniquity; and by the fear of the LORD one departs from evil" (Proverbs 16:6).
- "The fear of the LORD leads to life, and he who has it will abide in satisfaction; He will not be visited with evil" (Proverbs 19:23).
- "By humility and the fear of the LORD are riches and honor and life" (Proverbs 22:4).
- "Do not let your heart envy sinners, but be zealous for the fear of the LORD all the day; For surely there is a hereafter, and your hope will not be cut off." (Proverbs 23:17-18).

To deny to children the fear of God—and the blessings it brings in life—is at best a grave sin of omission and, at worst, an intentional act of soul-endangering spiritual abuse. Jesus warned us to be very careful about the way in which we treat *little ones*. "It would be better for him if a millstone were hung around his neck and he were thrown into the sea," he said, "than that he should offend one of these little ones."[25]

THE RESPONSIBILITY FOR EDUCATION: PARENTS

Education is first and finally a familial matter. This is consistently affirmed in the Scriptures, both Old and New Testaments. The Apostle Paul instructed fathers not to "provoke" their children but to "bring them up in the training and admonition of the Lord."[26]

Likewise, the book of Deuteronomy declares,

> And these words which I command you today shall be in your heart. You shall teach them diligently to your children, and shall talk of them when you sit in your house, when you walk by the way, when you lie down, and when you rise

> up. You shall bind them as a sign on your hand, and they shall be as frontlets between your eyes. You shall write them on the doorposts of your house and on your gates.[27]

While parents are ultimately accountable to God for their children's education, they can delegate that instructional responsibility. In the Old Covenant, the priestly tribe of the Levites had special teaching functions within the community.[28]

While parents may delegate the education of their children to others, parents cannot be alienated from their rights as the final authority over their children's education. That is to say, the state cannot take away from the parents that which God has assigned to them: the responsibility to educate their children. All extra-parental educational assistance derives its authority from the parent's authority. Anyone who is engaged in the education of someone else's children does so *"in loco parentis"* (in the place of the parents).

The Scripture affirms the rights of parents and the duties to their covenant children under God:

- "Behold, children are a heritage of the LORD, the fruit of the womb is a reward. Like arrows are in the hand of a warrior; so are children of one's youth. Happy is the man who has his quiver full of them: they shall not be ashamed, but shall speak with their enemies in the gate" (Psalm 127:3-5). See also Genesis 33:5, 48: 8-9; Isaiah 8:18; Hebrews 2:13.

- "Train up a child in the way he should go, and when he is old, he will not depart from it" (Proverbs 22:6).

- "We will not hide them from their children, telling to the next generation to come the praises of the LORD which He commanded our forefathers to teach their children, so that the next generation would know them, even the children yet to be born, and they in turn would tell their children. Then they would put their trust in God and would not forget His deeds but would keep His commands" (Psalm 78:4-7).

- "Thus saith the LORD: Do not learn the way of the Gentiles; Do not be dismayed at the signs of heaven, For the Gentiles are dismayed at them" (Jeremiah 10:2).

- "And do not be conformed to this world, but be transformed by the renewing of your mind, that you may prove what is that good and acceptable and perfect will of God" (Romans 12:2).

PROMISES FOR CHRISTIAN PARENTS

Christian parents can stand upon the promises of God to perpetuate His covenant to their children. While the education of children is important as a matter of Christian duty, there is no perfect education that can guarantee their salvation. God can overcome even a bad educational experience by the power of His grace. As you pray for your children and grandchildren, remember these important Scriptures and claim their promises as your own.

- "Then Peter said to them, 'Repent, and let every one of you be baptized in the name of Jesus Christ for the remission of sins; and you shall receive the gift of the Holy Spirit. For the promise is to you and to your children, and to all who are afar off, as many as the Lord our God will call'" (Acts 2:38-39).

- "Believe on the Lord Jesus Christ, and you will be saved, you and your household" (Acts 16:31).

- "For the unbelieving husband is sanctified by the wife, and the unbelieving wife is sanctified by the husband; otherwise your children would be unclean, but now they are holy" (1 Corinthians 7:14).

- "And all your children shall be taught by the LORD; and great shall be the peace of your children" (Isaiah 54:13).

The Bible's pattern for education was, as we shall see, followed by America's founding generation, but that model has been dismissed by our public schools with tragic consequences. The next chapter offers an overview of the founding era heights from which we have fallen.

THE FOUNDERS AND EDUCATION

SAM KASTENSMIDT

He has been called the "schoolmaster to America"[1] and "the father of American scholarship and education."[2] In 1828, Noah Webster published the nation's first dictionary, *An American Dictionary of the English Language*, which powerfully illustrates the founding era's philosophy toward education.

This "schoolmaster to America" understood that a Christian education was essential to the preservation of liberty. In the preface to his lexical masterpiece, Webster declared,

> In my view, the Christian religion is the most important and one of the first things in which all children, under a free government, ought to be instructed ... No truth is more evident to my mind than that the Christian religion must be the basis of any government intended to secure the rights and privileges of a free people.[3]

Even further, Webster included the duty of religious instruction in his definition of a "good education":

> ... that series of instruction and discipline which is intended

> to enlighten the understanding, correct the temper, and form the manners and habits of youth, and fit them for usefulness in their future stations. To give children a good education in manners, arts and science, is important; to give them a religious education is indispensable; and an immense responsibility rests on parents and guardians who neglect these duties.[4]

Such reliance upon the tenets of Christianity as the core means of education was most certainly not the exception in early America. In fact, the first law governing education in America was passed in 1647 to ensure that young children would be capable of studying the truths of Scripture. This law, passed by the General Court of the Massachusetts Bay Colony, required towns of at least fifty households to appoint a person to instruct children on how to read and write. The law, known as the "Old Deluder Satan Act"[5] made "knowledge of the Scriptures" its chief aim:

> It being one chief project of that old deluder, Satan, to keep men from the knowledge of the Scriptures, as in former times by keeping them in an unknown tongue … and corrupted with false glosses of saint-seeming deceivers; and to the end that learning may not be buried in the grave of our forefathers, in church and commonwealth, the Lord assisting our endeavors … It is therefore ordered … to appoint one within their town to teach all such children as shall resort to him to write and read.[6]

In a law passed eight years later, the New Haven Code of 1655 imposed literacy requirements upon Connecticut residents, so that:

> … all their children, and apprentices as they grow capable, may through God's blessing, attain at least so much, as to be able duly to read the Scriptures, and other good and profitable printed books in the English tongue, being their native language, and in some competent measure, to understand the main grounds and principles of Christian Religion necessary to salvation.[7]

Similarly, a 1690 Connecticut law declared,

> This legislature observing that ... there are many persons unable to read the English tongue and thereby incapable to read the holy Word of God or the good laws of this colony ... it is ordered that all parents and masters shall cause their respective children and servants, as they are capable, to be taught to read."[8]

TEXTBOOKS IN THE FOUNDING ERA

One look at America's most popular textbooks during the founding era secures the fact that Christianity was considered vital to the education of America's youth. Among these books were Christian hymnals, the *New England Primer, McGuffey's Reader*, and the Bible itself.

The *New England Primer* was a tremendously influential book in eighteenth century America. Most of the nation's Founding Fathers would have been instructed with this book. Among its lessons is a section on "The Dutiful Child's Promises." The precepts of this section—taken almost verbatim from the Word of God—encourage children to make the following pledge:

> I will fear God, and honour the King; I will honour my father and mother; I will obey my superiours; I will submit to my elders; I will love my friends; I will hate no man; I will forgive my enemies and pray to God for them; I will as much as in me lies keep all God's Holy Commandments; I will learn my catechism; I will keep the Lord's Day Holy; I will reverence God's Sanctuary for our God is a consuming fire.[9]

The Primer was first published in 1690 and remained America's most popular textbook for more than one hundred years. During the eighteenth century, its popularity was exceeded only by the Holy Bible. Historians estimate that five million copies were distributed during an era when America's population barely reached four million people.[10] This would be like selling well over 300 million copies of a book during the twentieth century.

Thomas Jefferson, to whom many secularists attribute the foundations of the so-called "wall of separation between church and state," openly sought to include religious instruction in public schools. While serving as president of the Washington, D.C. school board, Jefferson authored the District's first plan for public education, including both the Bible and the *Watts Hymnal* as the primary books for the city's students.[11]

In the nineteenth and twentieth centuries, *McGuffey's Reader* replaced *The New England Primer* as the nation's most popular textbook. Though originally published in 1836—more than four decades after the ratification of the U.S. Constitution—this textbook did not shrink from offering an education that was saturated in biblical principles and religious instruction. In the opening foreword to his readers, author William McGuffey declared,

> The Christian religion is the religion of our country. From it are derived our prevalent notions of the character of God, the great moral governor of the universe. On its doctrines are founded the peculiarities of our free institutions.... The Ten Commandments and the teachings of Jesus are not only basic but plenary.[12]

The contents of *McGuffey's Reader* were replete with references to Scripture. One lesson instructed children: "At the close of the day, before you go to sleep, you should not fail to pray to God to keep you from sin and from harm.... [P]ut your trust in Him; and the kind care of God will be with you, both in your youth and in your old age."[13]

Certainly, secular revisionist historians would face a difficult challenge in explaining how such a book could have been embraced by even a *few* public schools while simultaneously contending that our founding generations sought to remove religion from education. These assertions crumble under the fact that *McGuffey's Reader* was officially recognized as a public school textbook in 37 states. Between 1836 and 1920, over 120 million copies were sold—placing it behind only the Bible and Webster's *Dictionary* in the list of America's best-selling books of all time.[14]

In 1993, the federal government paid tribute to William McGuffey—making special note that he believed "religion and education to be interrelated and essential to a healthy society."[15]

CHRISTIAN ROOTS OF HIGHER EDUCATION

Christianity was integral to education in the founding era. From the smallest of grammar schools to the greatest of universities, knowledge of Jesus Christ was the ultimate objective of all education in colonial America. Read for yourself the formulations used in the founding documents of these institutions.

The 1636 rules at Harvard University stated, "Let every student be plainly instructed and earnestly pressed to consider well the main end of life and studies to know God and Jesus Christ which is eternal life (John 17:3) and therefore to lay Christ in the bottom as the only foundation of all sound knowledge and learning."[16]

Yale University issued this charge to its students: "Above all, have an eye to the great end of all your studies, which is to obtain the clearest conceptions of Divine things and to lead you to a saving knowledge of God in his Son Jesus Christ."[17]

The College of William & Mary proclaimed that it was founded so that "the Christian faith may be propagated ... to the glory of God."[18]

The original charter of Dartmouth College explained that it was founded "for the education and instruction of youths ... in reading, writing, and all parts of learning which shall appear necessary and expedient for civilizing and Christianizing the children."[19]

The University of Pennsylvania's first two rules in its code of conduct prohibited students from using the Lord's name in vain and required mandatory attendance, "particularly at the time of prayers, and of the reading of the Holy Scriptures."

Columbia College specified that "no candidate shall be admitted into the College ... unless he shall be able to render into English ... the Gospels from the Greek."[20]

Reverend Jonathan Dickinson, the first president of Princeton University, declared, "Cursed be all that learning that is contrary to the Cross of Christ."[21] Princeton's second president, Reverend John Witherspoon, likewise delivered lessons proclaiming,

> He is the best friend to American liberty, who is most sincere and active in promoting true and undefiled religion, and who sets himself with the greatest firmness to bear down profanity and immorality of every kind. Whoever is an avowed enemy of God, I scruple not [do not hesitate] to call him an enemy of his country.[22]

Today, Princeton University still boasts about the educational legacy of Witherspoon: "The record of Princeton men who studied under Reverend John Witherspoon is outstanding, including President James Madison [primary author of the U.S. Constitution], Vice-President Aaron Burr, nine cabinet officers, 21 United States senators, 39 members of the House of Representatives, three justices of the Supreme Court, 12 governors, and numerous delegates to the Constitutional Convention."[23]

CLASSICAL CHRISTIAN EDUCATION & THE BIRTH OF LIBERTY

It is well beyond all serious debate that the most influential book during the founding era was the Holy Bible.

In 1988, Donald S. Lutz, a professor from the University of Houston, conducted a massive study to determine which sources were most often quoted or cited by the Founders. The study included more than 3,000 compositions written from 1760 to 1805. Professor Lutz discovered that 34 percent of all the citations in these writings were from the Bible—making Scripture more than four times as heavily cited as the next most popular source.[24]

It should not be too surprising to learn that 24 of the 56 signers of the Declaration of Independence held seminary degrees.[25]

In addition to their thoroughly Christian education, the founding generations sought to learn from past historical experiments and philosophic teachings. The unfolding of history has shown that the written world of ideas comes with serious and often devastating consequences.

Thucydides, perhaps the most revered historian of Greek antiquity, once wrote that "history is philosophy teaching by examples."[26] Indeed, today's generations need only to reflect upon the generational impacts that have been wrought by the ideas of men like Muhammad, Machiavelli, Hobbes, Nietzsche, Darwin, and others to discover the immense power of the written word.

Having witnessed the enormous influence of books and philosophy upon the world, the Founders understood that it was imperative for a Christian citizenry to be well educated in the prior affairs of mankind. Indeed, history's greatest minds—Christian and pagan—have recognized the importance of education in both shaping and preserving the happiness of a society.

Aristotle rightly explained, "All who have meditated on the art of governing mankind have been convinced that the fate of empires depends on the education of youth."[27]

Likewise, Saint Augustine—oft-considered the greatest theologian in the history of the Church—urged believers to educate themselves not only in Scripture, but in the many great classics of history—Plato, Aristotle, Plutarch, Thucydides, Cicero, and the like.

In his treatise, *On Christian Doctrine*, he professed that the content of all pagan books is "poor ... when compared with the knowledge of Holy Scripture," but still urged believers to study the lessons of history and embrace any valuable philosophic insights. "We are not only not to shrink from it," he wrote, "but to claim it for our own use."[28] Augustine argued that just as the Israelites had plundered the great treasuries of Egypt during the Exodus, so too must Christians plunder all that is valuable from pagan philosophers, leaving behind all that is useless.

With this understanding, when the Founders were called upon to craft the U.S. Constitution, they were not so foolish as to ignore the great lessons that God had delivered in both Scripture and history. James Madison, the primary architect of the U.S. Constitution, warned,

> A popular Government, without popular information, or the means of acquiring it, is but a prologue to a farce or a tragedy; or, perhaps both. Knowledge will forever govern ignorance, and a people who mean to be their own Governors, must arm themselves with the power which knowledge gives.[29]

In 1788, Noah Webster described the books that had consumed the minds of America's youth during the constitutional era. In addition to the Bible, Webster noted, "The collections which are now used consist of essays that respect foreign and ancient nations. The minds of youth are perpetually led to the history of Greece and Rome or to Great Britain; boys are constantly repeating the declamations of Demosthenes and Cicero..."[30]

This entire generation was intimately familiar with world history and the classics of antiquity.

Historian Isaac Kramnick explains that prior to the commencement of the Constitutional Convention, Madison had asked Thomas Jefferson to "send from Paris *crates* of books on world government, the law of nations, history, and political theory."[31] So as not to repeat mistakes, the Founders were intent on plundering the great treasury of wisdom that had accrued in the histories of distant nations.

Unquestionably, this knowledge of world history and classical philosophy helped to shape the conception of liberty during the nation's founding era. As the Founders sought to develop a system that would allow for self-governance, they considered the reflections of philosophers like Plato, who warned, "Tyranny is probably best established out of no other regime than democracy—

the greatest and most savage slavery out of the extreme of freedom."[32]

Due to this comprehensive education, our Founders were able to navigate through the pitfalls that had arisen in the other systems of governance. It was this education which led them to guard against the depraved passions of men—as expressed by Scripture and confirmed in history—by establishing a system of checks and balances to fend off the despotic impulses of men. In *The Federalist Papers*, which are largely credited with persuading the American people to adopt the Constitution, Madison wrote,

> It may be a reflection on human nature that such devises should be necessary to control the abuses of government. But what is government itself but the greatest of all reflections on human nature? If men were angels, no government would be necessary. If angels were to govern men, neither external nor internal controls on government would be necessary.[33]

It was this careful study of Scripture, history, and philosophy that gave birth to the United States Constitution—the most successful national compact in the history of the world. The brilliance of the document led Madison to declare that his "fellow Americans must perceive in the Constitution a finger of that almighty hand which has so frequently extended to our relief in the critical stages of our revolution." George Washington labeled the brilliance of the Constitution "little short of a miracle," and Jefferson called it "the wisest [government] ever presented to man."[34]

Even so, they understood that the preservation of American liberty could not be sustained by written declaration alone. The legacy of liberty and virtue was wholly dependent upon the education of future generations.

THE INTENTIONS OF OUR FOUNDERS

For President George Washington, "religious principle" was necessary to promote and sustain the public good. Washington, whose own childhood education was steeped in Christianity,[35] declared in his famed Farewell Address to the nation:

> Of all the dispositions and habits, which lead to political prosperity, religion and morality are indispensable supports.... [R]eason and experience both forbid us to expect that national morality can prevail in exclusion

> of religious principle.[36]

One year after the U.S. Constitution was ratified, Samuel Adams, the Father of the American Revolution, explained that religious education *must* play a vital role in the preservation of American liberty. In a letter explaining how America could "establish the permanent foundations of freedom and happiness," Adams wrote, "Let divines and philosophers, statesmen and patriots, unite their endeavors to renovate the age by impressing the minds of men with the importance of educating their little boys and girls, inculcating in the minds of youth the fear and love of the Deity."[37]

Benjamin Franklin argued that schools should "afford frequent opportunities of showing the necessity of a public religion ... and the excellency of the Christian religion above all others."[38]

John Jay, the nation's first Chief Justice of the U.S. Supreme Court, once proclaimed, "The Bible is the best of all books, for it is the word of God and teaches us the way to be happy in this world and in the next. Continue therefore to read it and to regulate your life by its precepts."

Gouverneur Morris, the most active participant in the Constitutional Convention, proclaimed, "Religion is the only solid basis of good morals; therefore, education should teach the precepts of religion, and the duties of man towards God."[39]

Lest anyone claim that these men held aberrant views, it is worth noting that the entire U.S. Congress approved a measure urging the state to *forever* encourage the instruction of religion and morality. The Northwest Ordinance of 1787 emphatically declares, "Religion, morality, and knowledge, being necessary to good government and the happiness of mankind, schools and the means of education shall forever be encouraged."[40]

Even the U.S. Supreme Court made its opinion known in the case of *Vidal v. Girard's Executors* (1844). A unanimous Court explained:

> Why may not the Bible, and especially the New Testament, without note or comment, be read and taught as a divine revelation ... its general precepts expounded, its evidences explained, and its glorious principles of morality inculcated? Where can the purest principles of morality be learned so clearly or so perfectly as from the New Testament?[41]

Though modern secularists have made repeated attempts to repackage the spirit of the founding era, the writings and speeches of our Founding Fathers all testify against such claims. Even today, an official exhibit of the Library of Congress professes,

> The first national government of the United States was convinced that the "public prosperity" of a society depended on the vitality of its religion. Nothing less than a "spirit of universal reformation among all ranks and degrees of our citizens," Congress declared to the American people, would "make us a holy [people],that so we may be a happy people."[42]

Perhaps better than anyone else, Benjamin Rush, signer of the Declaration of Independence, captured the prevailing sentiments of our Founders: "The only foundation for a useful education in a republic is to be laid in religion. Without this there can be no virtue, and without virtue there can be no liberty, and liberty is the object and life of all republican governments."[43]

Unquestionably, America's founding was saturated with Christianity. Meanwhile, across the Atlantic Ocean, Europe was experiencing the so-called Enlightenment (or the "Age of Reason")—bringing great turmoil due to the emergence of empty atheistic philosophies which questioned man's ability to know the truth.

In his pamphlet, *Information to Those Who Would Remove to America*, Benjamin Franklin advised prospective immigrants from Europe:

> [B]ad examples to youth are more rare in America, which must be a comfortable consideration to parents. To this may be truly added, that serious religion, under its various denominations, is not only tolerated, but respected and practiced. Atheism is unknown there; Infidelity rare and secret; so that persons may live to a great age in that country without having their piety shocked by meeting with either an Atheist or an Infidel.[44]

The founding era was largely insulated from the influence of the atheistic philosophies that had been plaguing a post-Reformation Europe. However, the poisonous philosophies of the so-called Enlightenment would eventually make their way into the public policies of America—changing the nation's view of education.

FROM THE FOUNDERS TO DEWEY: THE ROLE OF IDEAS

ANTHONY URTI

The Founders had a clearly defined view of education. They understood the biblical duty of parents to be the primary educators of children. Today, this view of education has been largely turned on its head. No doubt, if such a view was presented to the National Education Association (NEA), it would be quietly dismissed as outmoded and archaic.

When did the transition from a Christian-based understanding of education to the current secularist view of public education take place?

KANT, ROUSSEAU, AND THE ENLIGHTENMENT

The founding of America was an experiment in the application of Christian thought to the political sphere. In the words of French historian Alexis de Tocqueville, America had developed a "wholly novel theory" and "a great discovery in modern political science."[1]

This radical view, which asserted that all men were created with "certain inalienable rights," originated in Scripture.[2] And yet, even amid the display of religious fervor, which aided significantly in the founding of America, there was already a philosophic movement afoot that would eventually move society away from the Bible and its lessons on education.

Much has been written on the age of the European Enlightenment.

Generally speaking, it was an eighteenth century movement in which many began to believe that the power of human reason could liberate and perfect the human race. As late missionary and theologian Lesslie Newbigin wrote, "Developments which had been ongoing for several centuries seemed to have reached a point of clarification such that people could only use the word 'enlightenment' to describe what had happened."[3] Indeed, it seemed that all at once, society's reverence for Scripture had been tossed aside, replaced by an unwarranted faith in skeptical reason. This era has had profound implications for the modern Western predicament, especially modern education.

Immanuel Kant (1724-1804) is widely considered to be the last major philosopher of the Enlightenment era.[4] Kant grew up in a home that stressed Pietism—a reform movement within the Protestant Church emphasizing upright conduct and personal study above doctrinal heritage or theology.[5]

Kant rebelled against the orthodox teachings of the Church—attributing his "enlightenment" to eighteenth century empirical skeptic David Hume. Kant would write that reading Hume's materials caused him to awaken from what he considered "a dogmatic slumber."

In his skepticism, Kant doubted man's ability to know truth—particularly in matters of religion.

> As things now stand, much is lacking which prevents men from being, or easily becoming, capable of correctly using their own reason in religious matters ... I have placed the main point of enlightenment—the escape of men from their self-imposed immaturity—chiefly in matters of religion ... because religious incompetence is not only the most harmful but also the most degrading of all.[6]

Kant's supposed awakening from his "dogmatic slumber" led him into what is commonly called the critical period of his scholarly life, when he would write his most famous work, *A Critique of Pure Reason*, published in 1781.

Kant's major contribution to modern secularism was his distinction between what he believed to be two distinct realities—what he called the *noumena* and the *phemomena*. This split opened a chasm in epistemology—the study of how we know what we know. The *noumena* is essentially the thing in itself, which constitutes reality. So, for example, a parked car is, in reality, a car. It is something we can see and touch. On the other hand, Kant proposed that *phenomena* are the experiences we have of reality. Thus, *phenomena* were nothing more than the appearance of reality, which may or may not be reality in truth.

In the *Republic*, Socrates—like Kant—explained the concept of perceived reality when he described his cave of deception—a place where a captive audience is tricked into believing that shadows projected on a cave wall are true reality. However, unlike Kant, Socrates explains that there is a true reality beyond the shadows to be known. For Socrates, true reality is outside the cave. However, the captives have never seen true sunlight, and they are easily brainwashed into believing that mere shadows are reality, *noumena*. In truth, however, the shadows are nothing more than a perceived reality, *phenomena*. What Kant did was to argue that mankind can never be certain whether he is looking at shadows or reality.

The importance of this distinction may not at once be clear, but we can bring the issue into sharper focus. The Bible, as Christians well know, is the inspired Word of God. As the Westminster Shorter Catechism puts it, "The Word of God, which is contained in the Scriptures of the Old and New Testaments, is the *only* rule to direct us how we may glorify and enjoy [God]."[7] Christians believe that this is a true statement; not just "true for me," but true in reality. Kant's distinction opens up the door, however, for the objective Word of God to be placed into the realm of the *phemonena*—simply an experience for the individual, not an objective truth to which all of humanity is subject.

The implications of the abandonment of absolute truth ought to be clear. Standards that are objectively true can easily be brushed aside as mere experiences, and therefore non-binding on humanity. The Apostle Paul, writing in Romans, tells us that all people know the truth of God because God has revealed it to them.[8] We are responsible because we know it. Paul also tells us that we, as fallible human beings, "suppress the truth in unrighteousness." Ultimately, we can be assured that the denial of absolute truth is a spiritual matter.

Immanuel Kant, in his philosophy, gave intellectual ammunition to those who would seek to suppress the truth.

America's Founders were very much aware of this temptation, and they warned against it. In his Farewell Address, George Washington addressed the dangers of atheistic philosophies. He declared,

> Where is the security for property, for reputation, for life, if the sense of religious obligation desert the oaths which are the instruments of investigation in courts of justice? And let us with caution indulge the supposition that morality can be

> maintained without religion. Whatever may be conceded to the influence of refined education on minds of peculiar structure, reason and experience both forbid us to expect that national morality can prevail in exclusion of religious principle.[9]

Jean-Jacques Rousseau (1712-1778), the French enlightenment thinker, also had a profound impact on the modern education movement. Known as a "social contractarian" thinker, Rousseau took the biblical idea of original sin and turned it upside down—believing that man was born inherently good and that society was the corrupting influence.

In fact, it has been written that "[Rousseau] believed that people in the state of nature were innocent and at their best and that they were corrupted by the unnaturalness of civilization. In the state of nature, people lived entirely for themselves, possessed an absolute independence, and were content."[10]

This view of man's inherent goodness, not surprisingly, led Rousseau to postulate the social contract in different terms than previous philosophers. For Rousseau, each individual willingly gives up his right to self-govern, so that he may participate in establishing rules for all of society. Rousseau argued that these rules then formed a collective body with one will—the "general will."

Rousseau's "general will," as it turns out, would become the firm basis for socialism—with the government's determinations becoming "the true interest of what everyone wants whether they realize it or not."[11] In other words, the governing body tells the individual what is best for his or her life. Rousseau believed, "One must choose between making a man and making a citizen, because one cannot simultaneously make both."[12]

Rousseau was undoubtedly more interested in the latter.

Edward Younkins, a professor at Wheeling Jesuit University, notes that Rousseau's philosophies—both his view of men and his "general will" theory—essentially call for state-controlled education programs:

> Rousseau maintained that the state must control all schooling because the objective of schooling is to develop citizens who want only what the community (i.e., the general will) wants. Because mankind was infinitely perfectible, human failings could be eradicated by education. Rousseau wants to mold and socialize the individual through universal public education.[13]

Rousseau's view of government certainly inspired many proponents of America's public school system—many of whom openly argued that the power of government should trump the rights of parents in the effort to "mold and socialize" children.

NINETEENTH CENTURY THOUGHT

To be sure, Kant and Rousseau were not islands unto themselves. They had been influenced by those who came before them, and they certainly impacted those who followed.

Christian theologian and apologist Gordon Clark writes that the nineteenth century was characterized by two philosophic trends—mechanic scientism and the absolute idealism of German philosopher Georg Wilhelm Friedrich Hegel.[14]

Mechanic scientism was characterized by the belief that the scientific enterprise took precedence over all other methods of viewing mankind and the world in which we live. By dismissing the legitimacy of faith, this philosophy has had tremendous consequences in matters of religion and metaphysics.

On the other end of the spectrum, Hegel believed in "the progressive evolution of truth,"[15] contending that any particular truth must be connected to an all-inclusive and evolving truth before it can be deemed true. This was considered absolute idealism. Hegel wrote,

> The truth is the whole. The whole, however, is merely the essential nature reaching its completeness through the process of its own development. Of the Absolute it must be said that it is essentially a result, that only at the end is it what it is in very truth; and just in that consists its nature, which is to be actual, subject, or self-becoming, self-development.[16]

Rejecting the idea of eternal revealed truth, Hegel believed that all truth was evolving. Under such a philosophy, it would follow that mankind could never be certain of *any* truth. In his book, *Orthodoxy*, G.K. Chesterton (1874–1936), the famous Christian apologist, pointed out the irrationality of such thinking. His chapter, "The Suicide of Thought," explains,

> [The skeptic] will not entirely trust anything.... And the fact that he doubts everything really gets in his way when

> he wants to denounce anything. For all denunciation implies a moral doctrine of some kind; and the modern revolutionist doubts not only the institution he denounces, but the doctrine by which he denounces it.... As a politician, he will cry out that war is a waste of life, and then, as a philosopher, that all life is waste of time. A Russian pessimist will denounce a policeman for killing a peasant, and then prove by the highest philosophical principles that the peasant ought to have killed himself.... The man of this school goes first to a political meeting, where he complains that savages are treated as if they were beasts; then he takes his hat and umbrella and goes on to a scientific meeting, where he proves that they practically are beasts.... In his book on politics he attacks men for trampling on morality; in his book on ethics he attacks morality for trampling on men.... By rebelling against everything he has lost his right to rebel against anything.[17]

Needless to say, such an evolving view of truth is completely hostile to the Christian's belief in special revelation—that God, through the Holy Spirit, has made His truths known to us.

The philosophies of Rousseau, Kant, and Hegel profoundly impacted early American education. Rousseau's socialist-minded contract theory would help to pave the way for state-controlled common schools, while the philosophies of Kant and Hegel led educators to abandon the pursuit for any eternal truths in the greater questions of life.

In the mid-1800s, Horace Mann, Massachusetts' first secretary of the Board of Education, and Massachusetts Governor Edward Everett emerged as major proponents of state-controlled common schools.

Their fervent support for this idea came after visiting Europe to study the authoritarian model of Prussian schools. Interestingly, both Mann and Everett were enthusiastic students of none other than Hegel, whom we have already linked generally to Immanuel Kant.[18] Thus, it is not surprising that Horace Mann, the father of the common school movement, felt that government-controlled schools should abandon the deeper philosophic educations to focus on the more basic and standardized essentials. It was the first attempt to dumb-down America's classrooms.

By 1837, Horace Mann and Governor Everett had successfully lobbied to introduce common schools to the state of Massachusetts. It was "Mann's driving determination to create a system of effective, secular, universal education in the United States," according to the Public Broadcasting System.It would not be long before other states followed suit.

Mann believed that a stable, harmonious social and civic order rested on education, literacy and what PBS called "the inculcation of common public ideals."[19] The role of state-controlled education was such, Mann wrote, that "A republican form of government, without intelligence in the people, must be, on a vast scale, what a mad-house, without superintendent or keepers, would be on a small one."[20] While laudable in his goals, Mann's foundational worldview served to undermine the goals he had set forth.

For Mann, the pursuit of educational greatness could be sacrificed to mere common competency. As he wrote, "The scientific or literary well-being of a community is to be estimated not so much by possessing a few men of great knowledge, as its having many men of competent knowledge."[21]

In 1840, as the common-school movement was gaining steam, the famous French historian Alexis de Tocqueville published his second volume of *Democracy in America*, in which he issued a sobering, and perhaps prophetic, warning to those in America who sought to exchange the lofty prize of rigorous education for the mire of mediocrity. Tocqueville wrote,

> If the members of a community, as they become more equal, become more ignorant and coarse, it is difficult to foresee to what pitch of stupid excesses their selfishness may lead them; and no one can foretell into what disgrace and wretchedness they would plunge themselves ... [T]he time is fast approaching when freedom, public peace, and social order itself will not be able to exist without education.[22]

Ultimately, by abandoning the pursuit to cultivate students of "great knowledge," the common school movement initiated the long downward spiral of public education, which has since stripped the Scriptures—the very source of American liberty, as Noah Webster declared[23]—from its classrooms.

THE DAWN OF PRAGMATISM

Still, further philosophical changes were about to take hold, thanks to a man named William James, who sought to replace "absolute logic with pragmatic experience."[24] Pragmatism, for James, meant interpreting "each notion by tracing its respective practical consequences...."[25]

In plain English, pragmatism is the philosophy that says "if it works, do it." Modern culture is fraught with such pronouncements. This philosophy rules the playgrounds and the academic halls. So long as something works for you or me, we are free to pursue it with vigor—abandoning any concern for virtue or truth.

For James, as he put it, the "only test of probable truth is what works best in the way of leading us, what fits every part of life best and combines with the collectivity of experience's demands, nothing being omitted."[26] Machiavelli could not have said it better himself. Under pragmatism, the ends justify the means.

JOHN DEWEY

By the early twentieth century, atheistic and socialistic tendencies had already gained a subtle foothold in American education by way of the Enlightenment and the common-school movement. But in July 1932, any subtleties ceased when the National Education Association (NEA) appointed Dr. John Dewey, whom *Time Magazine* had labeled a "liberal philosopher, humanist," to be its honorary president for life.[27]

John Dewey took pragmatism—along with his own thoroughly atheistic worldview—and applied it to public education. A brief biography of Dewey portrays the man this way:

> A philosophy professor at Columbia University and the University of Chicago. A declared atheist who sometimes used religious terminology, Dewey was a Hegelian. Holding that truth [is always] in process; it is never eternally fixed. Morals changed, he believed, as society changed.[28]

In other words, Dewey not only thought pragmatically—in the tradition of Hegel and James—he also thought progressively, as in "mankind is in route to being perfected in the here and now." Rousseau's impact looms large in the philosophy of Dewey.

One year after being named the NEA's honorary president, Dewey became one of the most prominent signers of the notorious *Humanist Manifesto*—an unabashedly atheistic treatise. This *Manifesto* declared,

> Religious humanists regard the universe as self-existing and

> not created.... [T]he nature of the universe depicted by modern science makes unacceptable any supernatural or cosmic guarantees of human values.... The time has passed for theism ... The religious forms and ideas of our fathers no longer adequate, the quest for the good life is still the central task for mankind. Man is at last becoming aware that he alone is responsible for the realization of the world of his dreams, that he has within himself the power for its achievement.[30]

The empty philosophy of humanism attempted to strip mankind of eternal purpose and eliminate absolute standards of right and wrong. Unquestionably, this agenda stood in complete contrast to the truths of Scripture and the pillars of America's heritage.

Dewey believed that it was "the business of the school" to serve as the primary engine toward social reform. As such, Dewey sought to produce a generation of Americans that would cling to the precepts of his humanist worldview. Such open hostility toward the precepts of the Christian faith was not entirely uncommon during this time. After all, this is the same era that produced Roger Baldwin (founder of the ACLU) and Margaret Sanger (founder of Planned Parenthood).

Like Baldwin, much of Dewey's support came from devotees of Marx, Lenin, and Stalin. During this period, intellectual elites would often make the long trek to the Soviet Union to observe atheistic government in action. Most returned with nothing but praise for Communism for "giving Soviet citizens universal suffrage, civil liberties, the right to employment, free education, free medical care, and material security in old age."[31] Of course, world history has proven them wrong. *The Black Book of Communism*, which catalogues the terror imposed by communist states, reports that a stunning total of 94 million people were killed under communist regimes in the twentieth century.[32]

Dewey argued that it was not the Church or the family, but the state-controlled school that should become the primary instrument of social reform. In his essay, *My Pedagogic Creed*, Dewey declared,

> I believe that education is the fundamental method of social progress and reform.... [I]t is the business of every one interested in education to insist upon the school as the primary and most effective instrument of social progress

> and reform.... Through education, society can formulate its own purposes...and thus shape itself...in the direction in which it wishes to move.[33]

Dewey's disregard for transcendent truth and his assertion that education was the "primary and most effective instrument of social progress and reform," became holy writ for a generation of academics who, in turn, stamped these ideas upon public school teachers and by extension, their young impressionable students in the classroom.

This pragmatic progressivism (seen in educational fads, such as "outcome-based education") became the foundation for a politicized educational system in which the Bible is no longer allowed. Tolerance of all viewpoints (except that of Christianity) is required, and educational mediocrity has ensued—all largely due to the philosophies of men like James and Dewey.

THE ESTABLISHED RELIGION OF SECULAR HUMANISM

Public education is, today, a monopoly that has become a powerful weapon in the hands of secular humanists. Charles F. Potter, a member of the NEA and a signer of the 1933 *Humanist Manifesto*, believed that humanism's influence in schools would ultimately lead to the collapse of Christianity as the dominant worldview in America. Potter wrote,

> Education is thus a most powerful ally of Humanism, and every American public school is a school of Humanism. What can the theistic Sunday schools, meeting for an hour once a week, and teaching only a fraction of the children, do to stem the tide of a five-day program of humanistic teaching?[34]

Sadly, Potter was right. Secular humanism *has* become the "established religion" in America's public schools—complete with an allergic aversion to God and a disdain for moral absolutes.

In 1961, the U.S. Supreme Court even referred to secular humanism as a religion. In a footnote to its decision in *Torcaso v. Watkins*, the Court declared, "Among *religions* in this country which do not teach what would generally be considered a belief in the existence of God are Buddhism, Taoism, Ethical Culture, *Secular Humanism* and others."[35] Yet this *religion* continues to be taught unabated in our public schools.

It is not a matter of *whether* religion is to be taught in the public schools. Rather, the real question must always be *whose* religion will be taught. It is absolutely impossible to teach about the world without religious implications. In modern public education, it should be quite obvious that the *religion* of Secular Humanism has replaced Christianity as the dominant religious worldview presented to our children. Or in simpler terms, Dewey's "*religious humanists*" have dethroned America's Christians as the shepherds of our future generations.

Though Christians have failed to recognize the great consequences of surrendering the public schools, those in the humanist camp understand the battle all too well.

A 1983 edition of *The Humanist* magazine ominously declared,

> [T]he battle for humankind's future must be waged and won in the public school classroom by teachers who correctly perceive their role as the proselytizers of a new faith: a religion of humanity … There teachers must embody the same selfless dedication of the most rabid fundamentalist preacher, for they will be ministers of another sort, utilizing a classroom instead of a pulpit to convey humanist values in whatever subject they teach … The classroom must and will become an arena of conflict between the old and the new—the rotting corpse of Christianity, together with all its adjacent evils and misery, and the new faith of humanism, resplendent in its promise of a world in which the never-realized Christian ideal of "love thy neighbor" will finally be achieved.[36]

The vast majority of public school teachers would likely reject such a venomous declaration. Yet it is irrelevant whether educators *willingly* operate under the banner of humanism. The framework of modern public education—shaped by judicial precedents and burdensome bureaucracy—now forces teachers to abide by the precepts of its new religion—secular humanism.

In the past fifty years, the U.S. Supreme Court has issued a flurry of court decisions calling for the secularization of the nation's public schools. These decisions have banned school prayer (1962),[37] Bible reading (1963),[38] a law prohibiting the teaching of Darwinian evolution (1968),[39] Ten Commandments displays (1980),[40] moments of silence (1985),[41] creationism lessons (1987),[42] nativity scenes (1989),[43] graduation prayer (1992),[44] scholarships for theology students (2003),[45] and more.

Who could honestly deny that secular humanism has become the established religion of America's public schools? Consequently, the public schools—rather than giving students a solid foundation for education—have become the chief proponents of this "new faith" and, as Dewey hoped, the most effective engines of social change.[46]

MEASURING THE DECLINE

SAM KASTENSMIDT

In launching the "common school" movement, Horace Mann promised, "The scientific or literary well-being of a community is to be estimated not so much by possessing a few men of great knowledge, as it's having many men of competent knowledge."[1]

Sadly for us, the common school movement has yielded neither result. On the contrary, as public education grows increasingly divorced from its historical roots of rigorous biblical and classical studies, the consequences have been disastrous.

THE DUMBING DOWN OF AMERICA

In 1981, at the behest of President Ronald Reagan, Secretary of Education Terrence Bell created the National Commission on Excellence in Education—directing the agency to examine the quality of public education in the United States. Two years later, the Commission published its findings, offering a scathing indictment of America's public schools. The report, *A Nation at Risk*, declares,

> If an unfriendly foreign power had attempted to impose on America the mediocre educational performance that exists

> today, we might well have viewed it as an act of war. As it stands, we have allowed this to happen to ourselves.... We have, in effect, been committing an act of unthinking, unilateral educational disarmament.[2]

In the year this report was published, American taxpayers had spent $215 billion on K-12 public education. After reviewing the report, President Reagan announced to the American people:

> We spent more on education at all levels than any other country in the world. But what have we bought with all that spending? ... Almost uninterrupted decline in student achievement...during the past two decades, decades in which the federal presence in education grew and grew. Today's high school graduates score almost 40 points below their 1963 counterparts on standard mathematic tests and 50 points lower on verbal tests.[3]

President Reagan called for the decentralization of public education and the abolition of the Department of Education—returning control back to local communities and parents. Unfortunately, Reagan's ambition failed to materialize.

In 1990, the U.S. Department of Education once again commissioned a review of public education in America. The National Assessment of Educational Progress (NAEP) published *The Nation's Report Card*, once again exposing the tremendous failures of public education. The downward trends had continued.

> Large proportions, perhaps more than half, of our elementary, middle, and high-school students are unable to demonstrate competency in challenging subject matter in English, mathematics, science, history, and geography. Further, even fewer appear to be able to use their minds well.[4]

LOSING OUR ABILITY TO READ

In 1998, the nation's *Reading Report Card* showed that the literacy levels of high school seniors had continued to decline through the 1990s.[5] In 2006, the Alliance for Excellent Education released a report estimating that up to six million middle and high school students are unable to read at acceptable levels. Among college-bound students who took the ACT exam, the majority were deemed unprepared for college-level reading.[6]

Consequently, even college graduates are now failing to demonstrate basic reading skills. In 2005, the National Center for Education Statistics reported that proficiency in reading among college graduates is in rapid decline. Michael Gorman, president of the American Library Association, admitted, "It is appalling—it's really astounding. Only 31 percent of college graduates can read a complex book and extrapolate from it. That's not saying much for the remainder."[7]

As a result, fewer and fewer Americans engage the great literary classics that helped to shape and inform all previous generations. A 2004 study conducted by the National Endowment for the Arts confirmed that "literary reading is in dramatic decline ... with the steepest rate of decline—28 percent—occurring in the youngest age groups."[8]

Dana Gioia, chairman of the National Endowment for the Arts, warned in the study's preface:

> For the first time in modern history, less than half of the adult population now reads literature, and these trends reflect a larger decline in other sorts of reading. Anyone who loves literature or values the cultural, intellectual, and political importance of active and engaged literacy in American society will respond to this report with grave concern.... America can no longer take active and engaged literacy for granted.... As more Americans lose this capability, our nation becomes less informed, active, and independent-minded. These are not qualities that a free, innovative, or productive society can afford to lose.[9]

Indeed, this preface only echoes the repeatedly expressed observations of our Founding Fathers. Men like Thomas Jefferson understood that education was absolutely essential for the future of our self-governing republic. "If a nation expects to be ignorant and free," wrote Jefferson, "it expects what never was and never will be."[10]

The consequences of the centralized "common school" movement have been ruinous. Indeed, the results of public education are thoroughly deplorable—especially when presented next to the brilliant minds generated in the Founding era. Indeed, much has changed since the days when Noah Webster wrote, "The minds of youth are perpetually led to the history of Greece and Rome or to Great Britain; boys are constantly repeating the declamations of Demosthenes and Cicero..."[11]

FAILING TO GRASP "BASIC GEOGRAPHIC LITERACY"

The vast majority of today's young people know absolutely nothing of Demosthenes or Cicero, and—in all likelihood—they could not even point to Greece or Rome on a map. A 2006 National Geographic study found that nearly two-thirds of Americans (ages 18-24) were unable to identify the United Kingdom on a world map. America's youth were not only geographically illiterate on a global scale; most young Americans were unable to identify the state of Ohio on a map.[12]

The National Geographic Education Foundation concluded,

> These results suggest that young people in the United States—the most recent graduates of our educational system—are unprepared for an increasingly global future. Far too many lack even the most basic skills for navigating the international economy or understanding the relationships among people and places that provide critical context for world events.... By and large, majorities of young adults fail at a range of questions testing their basic geographic literacy.[13]

FAILING TO GRASP MATHEMATICS

In 2003, the Organization for Economic Cooperation and Development (OECD) in Paris released the results of its Program for International Student Assessment (PISA). In this report, the OECD was able to assess and rank the educational development of students from leading nations.[14]

Though the United States now spends more money per pupil than any other nation besides Switzerland, our public education system proved abysmal in world competition. In an examination of 15-year-old students in the areas of mathematics and problem solving skills, the U.S. ranked 24th in a list of 29 participating nations.

One year after the international assessment, the Brookings Institution released a report, noting that most public school mathematics teachers are simply not prepared to teach their subject. The report explained,

> A majority of middle school math teachers do not have a standard teaching certificate in mathematics. Nor do they have an undergraduate degree in the subject.... Internationally, 71% of teachers of eighth grade mathematics hold bachelor's degrees in mathematics. In the U.S., only 41% hold math degrees.... Deficiencies in content knowledge have significant implications for the professional development of math teachers.[15]

According to a report conducted by Horizon Research,

> The National Council of Teachers of Mathematics has recommended that middle school mathematics teachers have college coursework in abstract algebra, geometry, calculus, probability and statistics, applications of mathematics/problem solving, and history of mathematics.... [Yet] roughly one out of every four middle school mathematics teachers has not had *any* of the six recommended mathematics courses.[16]

FAILING IN AMERICAN HISTORY AND CIVICS

The failures of public education extend into the realm of American history and civics as well. An August 2006 Zogby poll found that nearly three-quarters of Americans could name each of the Three Stooges (Moe, Larry, and Curly), while less than half could name the three branches of government (legislative, executive, and judicial). Likewise, the poll found that 77 percent of Americans could name two of the seven dwarfs, while just 24 percent could name two of the nine Supreme Court Justices.[17]

One month later, the Intercollegiate Studies Institute, in conjunction with the University of Connecticut's Department of Public Policy, released a study exploring whether the nation's schools were providing students with the necessary education to become responsible citizens. The report, "The Coming Crisis in Citizenship: Higher Education's Failure to Teach America's History and Institutions," examined "the state of learning about America's history and institutions on campuses throughout the nation."

"The results are far from encouraging," declares the report. "In fact, they constitute nothing less than a coming crisis in American citizenship.... Overall, college seniors failed the civic literacy exam, with an average score of 53.2

percent, or F, on a traditional grading scale."[18]

The study found that most college freshmen emerged from high school with a severe lack of basic knowledge about key components of any quality civics education. Most freshmen were completely unable to offer any explanation of the Founders' view of politics or morality. A majority of these freshmen were also unable to answer basic questions about the Declaration of Independence, the Bill of Rights, the origin of the doctrine of separation of church and state, federalism, or alternative forms of government.[19]

Interestingly, though it is quite obvious that the Founders' visions are lost in modern education, the study did find that a majority of students were able to answer questions about *Roe v. Wade* and the United Nations.

PRODUCING SCIENTIFICALLY ILLITERATE KIDS

For centuries, America has been a world leader in scientific and technological developments. From the cotton gin and the telephone to the airplane and the personal computer, America is the world's most innovative country. Unfortunately, modern trends show that the educational decline is beginning to place our nation on a much different trajectory.

In 2007, the U.S. Department of Energy's Office of Science entered the fray, warning that modern failures in public education may prove disastrous for America's positioning in an increasingly global economy. In its report, *Building a 21st Century Workforce*, the agency warned,

> Our Nation is failing to produce both a scientifically literate citizenry and the kind of workforce we will need in the 21st Century....Test scores from the Third International Mathematics and Science Study (TIMSS) placed the U.S. participants near the bottom of the 16 countries that administered the physics and advanced mathematics tests....[Consequently], from 1986-1999, 120,000 foreign students made up about 45% of the U.S. doctoral degree recipients in science and engineering.[20]

INSULATED MINDS AND GROWING EGOS

Study after study only confirms the wretched performance of public schools in a wide variety of subjects, including reading, mathematics, history, civics, geography, and science. Despite the precipitous decline in academics, both students and teachers refuse to acknowledge that we are underachieving.

The "self-esteem movement" has insulated today's schools from any criticism—constructive or otherwise. Indeed, many schools refuse to allow basic competition or academic rankings, fearing that some children might have their feelings hurt.

Thus, it is not surprising to learn that today's average college student—while less educated than students of previous generations—is now far more narcissistic and self-centered. In 2006, researchers from San Diego State University gathered responses from over 16,000 college students who participated in the Narcissistic Personality Inventory test. College students were asked to respond to statements like: "If I ruled the world, it would be a better place," "I think I am a special person," and "I can live my life any way I want to."[21]

The results confirmed what most sociologists already expected. The NPI scores only continued their steady climb—a trend which has been in place since the test was first introduced in 1982. Professor Jean Twenge, the study's lead author, stated, "We need to stop endlessly repeating 'You're special' and having children repeat that back. Kids are self-centered enough already."

Unfortunately, the modern education establishment remains unwilling to admit that there are serious problems in public education. Most teachers are now insulated from accountability and academically ill-equipped to teach. Consequently, children are simply shuffled from grade to grade without any true challenges or significant educational development.

Rather than claiming responsibility for these failures and vowing to move in a new direction, the establishment blames its problems on a supposed lack of funding. In the 23 years since *A Nation at Risk* was first published, Americans have spent *trillions* on public education. Annual funding for public schools has gone from $215 billion to $536 billion; and still our nation's schools continue to fail.

FUNDING IS NOT THE PROBLEM

The average U.S. class size is smaller than international norms, while American teachers make more than their international counterparts. Nevertheless, many nations with bigger classes and teachers who make less routinely generate better students. Yet proponents of the status quo insist that the failures of public schools are attributable to a lack of funding.

Even apart from international analysis, experience shows that this argument holds no merit.

In his book, *Money and School Performance*, Paul Ciotti highlighted the failures of the nation's most well-funded school district. In 1985, U.S. District Judge Russell Clark ordered the state of Missouri to spend $2 billion over a 12-year span to "improve" conditions in Kansas City schools. Consequently, the dramatic increase in funding was used for the construction of new schools, renovation of old ones, new state-of-the-art technologies, increased teacher salaries, and programs to bring student test scores in line with national averages.[22]

At the time of the decision, public education activists promised that the court's decision would ultimately prove the universal need for increased funding. However, this 12-year experiment only showed that the quality of public education is not always tied to funding.

"It was a major embarrassment and an ideological setback for backers of vastly increased funding for public schools," Ciotti explained.

> For more than a decade, the Kansas City district got more money per pupil than any other of the 280 major school districts in the country. Yet in spite of having perhaps the finest facilities of any school district its size in the country, nothing changed. Test scores stayed put, the three-grade-level achievement gap between blacks and whites did not change, and the dropout rate went up, not down.[23]

Despite the tremendous boost in funding, the district performed so poorly that it actually lost its accreditation with the state.[24]

This case is not an aberration; it is a national trend! The U.S. Department of Education estimated that roughly 48 million students were enrolled in the nation's public schools (grades K-12) in 2005.[25] During that year, total spending on public schools reached $536 billion—equating to more than $11,000 per child.[26] Public spending per student nearly quadrupled in the years since 1970,[27] yet SAT scores and almost every measurable standard of performance declined.[28] Still, many are quick to blame these problems on a lack of adequate funding.

Meanwhile, the U.S. Department of Education reports that the average annual K-12 private school tuition in 2004 was only $6,900.[29] Though private schools are typically forced to operate with less funding per pupil and smaller teacher salaries, studies now show that privately schooled children excel in virtually all aspects of education.

In 1992, William Bennett, former U.S. Secretary of Education, pointed to the success of private schools. "Christian academies [and] little Catholic schools in the inner city ... run at about one-third of the cost of the public schools, but produce a much better result."[30]

The National Center for Education Statistics (NCES), a division of the Department of Education, compared the results of private versus public schooling in a July 2006 report. It found that, "In grades 4 and 8 for both reading and mathematics, students in private schools achieved at higher levels than students in public schools."[31] Unfortunately, in a clear attempt to bring public schools toward parity, the study went on to make unilateral statistical adjustments to account for family income, student backgrounds, and inner city children.[32]

Regardless, the government's research testifies against the effectiveness of its own programs. When it comes to both controlling costs and achieving results, private schools outperform public schools in nearly every measurable category.

REFUSAL OF ACCOUNTABILITY

In January 2006, John Stossel, an investigative reporter and co-anchor for ABC's *20/20*, hosted a television special titled "Stupid in America: How We Cheat Our Kids." Stossel pointed out:

> The longer kids stay in American schools, the worse they do in international competition. They do worse than kids from poorer countries that spend much less money on education, ranking behind not only Belgium but also Poland, the Czech Republic, and South Korea. This should come as no surprise if you remember that public education in the United States is a government monopoly. Don't like your public school? Tough. The school is terrible? Tough. Your taxes fund that school regardless of whether it is good or bad. That is why government monopolies routinely fail their customers.[33]

After this special was aired to a nationwide audience, teachers' unions were furious. How dare anyone accuse the public schools of poor performance? Hundreds of angry protesters rallied outside of ABC's headquarters demanding an apology from ABC, *20/20*, and Stossel himself.[34]

Of course, the protesters did not bother to offer evidence refuting Stossel's claims. Rather, the leading defenders of public education—namely the teachers' unions—only showed a complete unwillingness to accept any responsibility for the system's massive failures.

This is not to say that these teachers' unions speak for all teachers. Certainly there are many excellent teachers in the public schools who recognize the existing problems.

Dr. D. James Kennedy, president and founder of Coral Ridge Ministries, has often praised the work of Christian teachers in America's public and private schools.

> There are those educators who have thought life through from a Christian perspective. They approach all of reality with Christ and the Bible as the center of their lives. All they teach, by both their words and their deeds, is affected by their Christian faith and philosophy. It is these teachers who hold the key to recovering the American education system.... These Christian teachers are the salt which remains in the public schools, and it is mainly through them that reform can occur. Many of these teachers perceive the public schools as their mission field and have been reaching out to young people for years.[35]

Despite the best efforts of Christian teachers in the public schools, the late Milton Friedman, recipient of the Nobel Prize in economics and senior research fellow at the Hoover Institution, insisted that America's increasingly centralized and insulated education model is doomed to fail, because it lacks both competition and accountability—ingredients that are key to the success of any enterprise. Friedman explained,

> The quality of schooling is far worse today than it was in 1955 .... The reason is partly ... the increased centralization of public schools—as evidenced by the decline in the number of school districts from 55,000 in 1955 to 15,000 in 1992 .... The system over time has become more defective as it has become more centralized. Power has moved from the local community to the school district to the state, and to the federal government. About 90 percent of our kids now go to so-called public schools, which are really not public at all but simply private fiefs primarily of the

> administrators and the union officials.[36]

In an interview with Dr. Kennedy that aired on *Truths That Transform*, former education secretary William Bennett urged Americans to get behind measures—namely school vouchers—that would decentralize the nation's educational system. "This very simple measure of giving parents the say would take power away from the unions, from the establishment, from the bureaucracy, and put it where it belongs—in the hands and feet of the American people."[37]

Dr. Kennedy agrees, "One of the great glories of American education is that it has historically been under the control of parents and concerned citizens in the local community."[38]

As the primary responsibility for education shifts away from parents and churches toward government and teacher unions, public education has become intensely politicized—with its leading voices determined to maintain a stranglehold on public education. Thus, while the NEA may not be able to brag about public school performance, it can certainly boast of being "one of the most powerful lobbying organizations" in America.[39]

To put it simply: without standards of accountability and a competitive environment, public schools are left with no incentives to pursue improvement. Under the current system, the most incompetent of public school teachers faces no real threat to job security, and the teacher unions continue to oppose standards of accountability. In fact, the NEA endorsed a resolution declaring that "competency testing must not be used as a condition of employment, license retention, evaluation, placement, ranking, or promotion of licensed teachers."[40]

The nation's largest teachers' union considers *competency* to be an overly burdensome requirement for the employment, evaluation, or promotion of public school teachers.

This is a problem!

And while virtually all analyses show that the nation is facing an educational crisis, Reg Weaver, president of the NEA, insists that schools "are doing an outstanding job."[41]

A *Wall Street Journal* opinion article highlighted the widespread problem of denial and the rejection of accountability standards among public school proponents. David S. Hahn explained,

> The average American receives a pretty mediocre education.

> The average SAT score drifted down from 1000 in the 1960s to 880 in 1993. Education activists attributed this plummet to cultural factors, a change in the testing pool, and other matters. The blame was placed everywhere but on schools. That the quality of education in America declined from the 1960s to the 1990s was hardly noted.[42]

THE FAILURE OF PUBLIC SCHOOL LEADERSHIP

In March 2005, Arthur E. Levine, the peer-respected president of Teachers College at Columbia University, released a 140-page report, criticizing the modern university programs which are designed to train up effective school administrators. Levine explained that the modern programs appeared to be in "a race to the bottom" with quality ranging "from inadequate to appalling."[43]

Two years earlier, Fordham Institute published a similar report, "Better Leaders for America's Schools: A Manifesto." Its sponsors included two former U.S. Secretaries of Education, two governors, one U.S. Senator, presidents from numerous think tanks, four state commissioners of education, the former head of the College Board, and director of the Council of Great City Schools.[44]

Unlike the teachers' unions, these leading officials refused to deny the obvious, agreeing that America's public schools are in serious trouble. The officials recognized a need for the public school system—at every level—to break the public education "cartel" of bureaucracies and unions that have prevented progress and kept talented people from reaching leadership.

Likewise, the panel insisted that "teachers should be held accountable for classroom-level results."

The "Manifesto" concluded,

> The United States is approaching a crisis in school leadership. For at least a generation, as American public education has stagnated, the conventional wisdom about leadership has focused on an old idea: certify educators to fix the problem. Today, two decades after we were pronounced a "nation at risk" as a consequence of the lackluster performance of our schools … too many of our schools turn out students who are ill equipped for the world in which they will work and live.[45]

AN EXAMPLE OF LEADERSHIP IN EDUCATIONAL EXCELLENCE

Parents and pastors must seek to reclaim the responsibility for education of youth from the State. Homeschooled and privately schooled children have not suffered the same precipitous declines in education that have so rampantly infected public schools. Thankfully, many parents and private institutions are offering outstanding educational opportunities for students.

In 1971, as secularism was spreading through the public schools, Dr. Kennedy, who is also pastor of Coral Ridge Presbyterian Church, founded a private Christian school in Fort Lauderdale, Florida. Noting that "true education has God alone at its center,"[46] Westminster Academy opened its doors, professing that it exists—not for its own ends—but rather "to serve Christian parents and their children."[47]

While SAT score averages have plummeted in public school institutions, SAT scores for the 101 graduating members of Westminster's class of 2005 averaged *over* 1100[48]—dramatically outperforming Florida's average SAT score, which remained *below* the 1000 mark.[49]

Unquestionably, the public school system is failing America's future generations. Thus, it is imperative for Christian parents to intervene.

"If parents cannot send their children to Christian schools or homeschool them and are forced to send them to public schools, they must commit themselves to a high involvement in their education,"[50] Dr. Kennedy has said. "Christ must rule over every thought, action, and plan—in every area of life. It is this vision of Christian education that we must pursue with all our hearts, minds, and souls. Imparting such a view to our children shall create, by God's grace, a Christian civilization as has never been seen in the history of the world.[51]

MORAL COLLAPSE

SAM KASTENSMIDT

Though virtually every measurable category of public education is in perceivable decline, the loudest public education debates have little to do with improving basic skills in math, literacy, or science. Rather, they center on highly charged cultural issues like sex education, the origin of man, and whether students should be permitted to pray at school events.

To put it plainly, public education has been consumed by controversies surrounding the moral upbringing of the next generation of Americans. Much has changed since the Founding Era, when the nation's most popular textbook instructed children: "You should not fail to pray to God."[1]

The Founders—the men who crafted the Constitution and believed "education should teach the precepts of religion and the duties of man towards God"—would be appalled that such education is now forbidden and deemed unconstitutional.[2]

In place of the Christian religion, America's entire public education system is now thoroughly saturated with the precepts of secular humanism. Alongside an activist judicial branch, America's teachers' unions have become the fiercest defenders of this national religious establishment of secular humanism in the public schools.

THE NATION'S LARGEST TEACHERS' UNION

In the decades since the National Education Association (NEA) elected Dr. John Dewey, a self-professing humanist, to be its honorary president for life, the organization has experienced monumental growth. In 2003, sixty-eight percent of all teachers belonged to the NEA[3]—making it the nation's largest labor union.

In recognition of the fact that the great majority of our children's teachers belong to this union, it would be prudent to gain a clear picture of the organization which claims to be "the voice of education professionals."

By its name alone, one would assume that the National Education Association is primarily concerned with matters of education. However, the slightest bit of research, or a quick review of its official handbook for teachers, shows that the NEA is little more than a political machine—using its public image and enormous clout to advance an ideologically driven social agenda that extends far beyond the scope of education.

Consider several of the resolutions which have been officially adopted by the NEA:

- "The NEA supports … reproductive freedom [abortion] without governmental intervention."[4]
- "The [NEA] … also urges the implementation of community-operated, school-based family planning clinics [e.g., Planned Parenthood]."[5]
- "[T]o facilitate the realization of human potential, it is the right of every individual to live in an environment of freely available information and knowledge about sexuality."[6]
- "[L]ocal school boards should adopt policies that govern religious activities on school property. Such policies must respect the separation of church and state."[7]
- "The Association also believes that the constitutional provisions … require that there be no sectarian practices in the public school program."[8]
- "[Sexual orientation] should not affect the legal rights and obligations of the partners in a legally recognized … civil union or marriage."[9]
- "[E]fforts to legislate English as the official language disregard cultural pluralism … and must be challenged."[10]
- "[S]trict proscriptive regulations are necessary for the

manufacture, importation, distribution, sale and resale of handguns."[11]

- "The Association urges its members to become politically involved and to support the political action committees [PACs] of the Association and its affiliates."[12]

The NEA handbook for education officials reads like a political party platform. While the NEA claims to be nonpartisan, an analysis of NEA Political Action Committee donations between 1977 and 1998 showed that over 95 percent of all campaign gifts went to candidates from just one political party.[13]

The NEA seems more interested in partisan politics than remedying the failing condition of public schools. Indeed, their own resolutions reveal that the NEA is unabashedly committed to advancing Dewey's social reforms through the public school classroom. For example, in March 2004, the NEA was listed as an official sponsor of the pro-abortion march in Washington, D.C.,[14] which was organized "to protect our right to abortion."[15]

How does an abortion rally improve education ... smaller class sizes?

While the NEA claims to be concerned about teachers' salaries, its own budget reflects no such concern. In 2005, the average teacher paid roughly $140 in annual dues to the NEA.[16] While the NEA complained about the status of underpaid teachers, the organization was milking teachers for dues and dishing out lavish salaries to its six hundred employees—salaries that averaged more than double the average salary of teachers. NEA president Reg Weaver received $439,000.

In 2006, of the $295 million collected from underpaid teachers, *The Wall Street Journal* reported that the NEA gave more than $65 million to a laundry list of radical organizations like the Human Rights Campaign (the nation's largest homosexual advocacy group), the Gay and Lesbian Alliance Against Defamation, People for the American Way (whose self-proclaimed mission is "to fight the Religious Right"[17]), Amnesty International, Jesse Jackson's Rainbow PUSH Coalition, and scores of others.

The *Journal* concluded that this southpaw-sided largesse exposes "the union as a honey pot for left-wing political causes that have nothing to do with teachers, much less students."[18]

While the NEA complains incessantly about teacher salaries, the organization has opposed the idea of merit-based pay raises.[19] The organization has repeatedly opposed measures to loosen the government's stranglehold on education or to impose basic competency standards for teachers. In 2004,

Rod Paige, then U.S. Secretary of Education, likened the NEA to "a terrorist organization" that engages in "obstructionist scare tactics" to prevent reforms in public education.[20]

Oftentimes, the speeches of leading NEA figures reveal that the organization's agenda goes far beyond mere politics. For example, in 1985, during a speech to the Kansas Educational Association Representative Assembly, Jim Lewis, a then-member of the NEA Executive Committee, declared,

> For 128 years, the NEA has been in the business of protecting its membership, and we cannot and will not turn aside from these responsibilities now. We have to go on the offensive. We have to go on the offensive against these evangelical bigots. We have to go on the offensive against these right-wing fanatics. And we have to go on the offensive against the political poltroons they have put in place and defeat them when they run for re-election to office.[21]

Likewise, at an annual conference for the Gay Lesbian Straight Education Network (GLSEN), Deanna Duby, associate director for NEA External Partnerships and Advocacy,[22] excited a largely homosexual audience by suggesting that the public schools are cultivating a generation that will reject traditional Christian values. "The fear of the religious right," she said, "is that the schools of today are the governments of tomorrow. And you know what? They're right."[23]

HOMOSEXUALITY IN PUBLIC SCHOOLS

The Gay Lesbian and Straight Education Network (GLSEN), though not widely known, has a rapidly growing presence in public education—particularly through the establishment of homosexual clubs in the schools. Since 2002, the presence of Gay Straight Alliance clubs (GSAs) in the nation's schools has grown from 1,200 to more than 3,000.[24] Kevin Jennings, executive director of GLSEN, has stated that they are "exploding across America."[25]

Alongside the growth of GSA clubs, GLSEN has conducted hundreds of workshops in the public schools to advance its agenda.

On March 25, 2000, GLSEN hosted a state-sponsored workshop in Massachusetts, which was held to increase the number of GSA clubs in the state's schools. The conference, titled "Teach Out," was designed for children as young as twelve, and it awarded "professional development credits" to teachers in attendance.

The conference delivered presentations that were nothing short of pornographic—and included public school officials describing the pleasures of homosexual sex. One official from the Massachusetts Department of Education went so far as to tell students, "Fisting often gets a bad rap.... [It is] an experience of letting somebody into your body that you want to be that close and intimate with."[26]

The materials and workshops available to faculty and students included topics like:

- "Ask the Transsexuals"[27]
- "Lesbian Avengers: How to Promote Queer Friendly Activism in Your Schools"
- "Diesel Dykes and Lipstick Lesbians: Defining & Exploring Butch/Femme Identity"
- "The Religious Wrong: Dealing Effectively with Opposition in Your Community"
- "Putting the 'Sex' Back Into Sexual Orientation"
- "It's Elementary in Our Town: Getting Gay & Lesbian Issues Included in Elementary School Staff Development"[28]

This is the same state where, just two years later, seven students were suspended from Westfield High School for distributing candy canes during the Christmas season.[29] Apparently, candy canes are too offensive for Massachusetts public schools, but not "diesel dykes."

On April 30, 2005, GLSEN made another splash at the GLSEN Boston Conference in Brookline, Massachusetts, by making a sexually explicit pamphlet, *The Little Black Book: Queer in the 21st Century*, available to its 500 attendees, mostly middle and high school students.[30] *Bay Windows*, a homosexual-oriented area newspaper, reported, "Once again, the annual conference of the Gay, Lesbian and Straight Education Network of Boston has become mired in controversy over exposing young people to sexually explicit materials."[31]

The pamphlet, which was displayed immediately after the registration table, included pornographic images, the vilest of language, and graphic sex tips for "queerboys."[32] The pamphlet also included an advertisement for 17 Boston area gay bars.

"Here is a list of Boston area bars and clubs for the discerning queerboy," stated the pamphlet before launching into the list of clubs—complete with addresses and descriptions such as: "sex-charged late at night," "strippers dancing," and "porn on the television."[33]

Sally Turner, an elderly woman who attended the conference, told a television reporter that she had "never seen anything so horrible in all of my life."[34] The materials were so disturbing that Massachusetts Governor Mitt Romney issued a statement: "Graphic pornographic material on the gay lifestyle has no place in any school.... [T]his particular publication is grossly inappropriate and should never find its way into the hands of school-aged children."

Not surprisingly, the NEA, which GLSEN considers to be "a key partner,"[35] actively refers school officials to GLSEN, suggesting that schools host workshops addressing homosexuality. One NEA resource even goes so far as to explain the circumstances in which schools can prevent religious students from presenting opposing viewpoints. The pamphlet explains,

> Some students have religious or moral objections to homosexuality and want a chance to provide a public counterpoint.... If a school itself provides information to students ... the school has greater control over that message.... In general, others have no right to present an opposing view within these official school activities.[36]

Unfortunately, government-controlled schools are becoming increasingly intolerant of divergent positions on moral issues of the day. The entire framework for modern schools is now geared to censor the beliefs of traditional Christians on a whole series of topics—ranging from evolution and philosophy to homosexuality and sex education.

CATERING TO HOMOSEXUAL STUDENTS

In 2002, Pioneer High School in Ann Arbor, Michigan, hosted a "Diversity Week" discussion panel titled "Homosexuality and Religion," in which students listened to various clergy members discussing religious views on homosexuality. On the surface, such an event might sound like an interesting discussion. However, school officials allowed this entire discussion panel to be set up by members of the school's Gay Straight Alliance (GSA).[37]

Not surprisingly, the GSA sought panel members with pro-homosexual views. As a result, Betsy Hansen, a senior at Pioneer High, objected and requested that the school invite someone to present the Roman Catholic perspective on homosexuality.

Incredibly, school officials rejected Hansen's request, explaining that a Roman Catholic representative might provide a "negative" viewpoint on homosexuality, which might "water down" the "positive" position that the school sought to convey—namely that homosexuality was compatible with major religions. As expected, after refusing to allow the Catholic perspective, the district then presented students with perspectives from six different clergy members (some in full garb), each presenting homosexuality as an acceptable alternative lifestyle.

In July 2002, on behalf of Hansen, the Thomas More Law Center filed a federal lawsuit against the school district, claiming that the school had violated her right to free speech and equal protection.

In December 2003, in a blistering yet refreshing 70-page court decision, U.S. District Judge Gerald E. Rosen slammed the district for its blatant double-standard and awarded over $102,000 in attorneys' fees to the Thomas More Law Center.[38] Judge Rosen declared,

> This case presents the ironic, and unfortunate, paradox of a public high school celebrating "diversity" by refusing to permit the presentation to students of an "unwelcomed" viewpoint on the topic of homosexuality and religion, while actively promoting the competing view.... The notion of sponsorship of one viewpoint to the exclusion of another hardly seems to further the school's purported objective of "celebrating diversity."[39]

While Christian teachers and students are consistently censored in the public schools, New York City education officials actually approved the creation of an entire school designed exclusively for the sake of homosexual students. After the city's board of education approved a $3.2 million renovation of the school's new building,[40] the Harvey Milk High School opened its doors as the "nation's first public high school for gays, bisexuals, and transgender students."[41]

Principal William Salzman told reporters, "This school will be a model for the country and possibly the world." Mike Long, an opponent of the proposed school, told reporters that it was nothing more than an attempt at "social engineering," asking, "Is there a different way to teach homosexuals? Is there gay math? This is wrong."[42]

City officials claimed that the taxpayer-funded school was necessary to provide a safe environment for gay students. Yet less than three months after its opening, five of its male students were arrested for impersonating undercover police officers while disguised as female prostitutes, in order to steal thousands in cash and credit cards from unsuspecting johns. In one robbery, three of the students held a man at gunpoint before taking $85 from his wallet.[43]

EVOLUTION — NO SCIENTIFIC CRITICISM ALLOWED

Albert Einstein once declared, "Science without religion is lame."[44] Einstein, perhaps the greatest scientist of the twentieth century, would be barred from sharing this belief inside America's public school classrooms.

A 2005 Harris poll revealed that the vast majority of Americans oppose the "evolution only" approach used in high school biology courses—with only 12 percent supporting it. Though 55 percent of Americans support the teaching of creationism, intelligent design, and evolution,[45] the nation's schools and courts have turned a deaf ear—refusing to allow any competing views. In fact, the education establishment has traditionally opposed any form of curriculum that exposes the weaknesses of Darwin's theory of origins.

DOVER, PENNSYLVANIA

In 2004, the Dover, Pennsylvania, school board voted 6-3 to adopt a policy stating, "Students will be made aware of gaps/problems in Darwin's Theory and of other theories of evolution including, but not limited to, Intelligent Design. Note: Origins of life will not be taught."[46]

In response, the Pennsylvania State Education Association assisted in efforts to overturn the policy,[47] claiming that teachers should not be required to teach a theory that is "not science." Tom Scott, an attorney retained by the teacher union, stated, "Unfortunately, the school board and the superintendent can put anything they want to in front of the students, but we are not going to be their messenger."[48]

On December 20, 2005, the Dover Area School Board lost its legal battle against the ACLU and the education establishment. U.S. District Judge John E. Jones III sided with the plaintiffs and issued a ruling that forbade the school board from adopting any curriculum that might "denigrate or disparage the scientific theory of evolution."

Judge Jones declared, "[I]t is unconstitutional to teach [intelligent design] as an alternative to evolution in a public school science classroom."[49] In an obvious attempt to intimidate other school districts around the nation, Judge Jones declared that the plaintiffs' attorneys were entitled to more than $2 million, though they agreed to settle for just over $1 million.[50]

COBB COUNTY, GEORGIA

In a similar case, the Cobb County, Georgia, school board merely decided to place factual labels inside of biology textbooks, advising students: "This textbook contains material on evolution. Evolution is a theory, not a fact, regarding the origin of living things. This material should be approached with an open mind, studied carefully, and critically considered."[51]

Despite the simple, limited nature of the sticker, evolution proponents mounted a massive legal campaign to have them removed. While no honest scientist who adheres to the scientific method could deny that Darwin's theory of origins is, indeed, just a theory, U.S. District Judge Clarence Cooper ordered the school district to remove the stickers, warning that the stickers might send "a message that the school board agrees with the beliefs of Christian fundamentalists and creationists."[52]

He continued,

> The sticker also has the effect of undermining evolution education to the benefit of those Cobb County citizens who would prefer that students maintain their religious beliefs regarding the origin of life.... Defendants shall immediately remove the sticker from all science textbooks into which the sticker has been placed.[53]

Sadly, as the public schools continue to teach that man is little more than a random mass of colliding cells, it will inevitably yield tragic consequences. If children view themselves as the accidental result of a random path of mutations from amoeba to man, then life will have no purpose or value. In a Darwinian world, there is no higher authority and no accountability beyond this life—leaving natural selection (only the strong survive) as the only logical system of justice. This worldview will invariably lead to tragedy.

COLUMBINE HIGH SCHOOL

Consider the tragic events at Columbine High School. Police reports reveal that as Eric Harris and Dylan Klebold carried out their plan to massacre students and teachers, Harris tore off his trench coat to expose a white T-shirt emblazoned with the words: "Natural Selection."[54] Shortly before the massacre, Harris made an ominous entry on his website, declaring, "YOU KNOW WHAT I LOVE??? Natural SELECTION! It's the best thing that ever happened to the Earth. Getting rid of all the stupid and weak organisms."[55]

Unquestionably, Harris had been greatly influenced by the teachings of Charles Darwin.

Shortly after the tragedy, the school asked the victims' families to design memorial tiles for a school wall. Yet when families designed tiles with religious inscriptions—like "Jesus Wept" and "God is Love"—the school district refused to display these tiles on school grounds.

The families filed a federal lawsuit, but the Tenth U.S. Circuit Court of Appeals declared that the school was correct to prohibit religious memorials. In a vacuum of both compassion and commonsense, the court explained,

> [W]e believe that the District's restriction on religious symbols was reasonably related to its legitimate goal of preventing disruptive religious debate on the school's walls. The District would be required to post tiles with inflammatory and divisive statements, such as "God is Hate," once it allows tiles that say "God is Love."[56]

ISLAM AND THE MULTICULTURAL BATTLE CRY

While Christian viewpoints are consistently censored in the public schools, other religions have not faced the same level of hostility. The Byron Union School District in California actually adopted an "Islamic Simulation" curriculum in which seventh graders were required to use Islamic names, wear a badge with the Islamic star and crescent moon, dress in Muslim garb, recite prayers, memorize verses from the Quran, memorize the five pillars of the Islamic faith, simulate Ramadan fasting, and play "Jihad games."[57]

In response, the Thomas More Law Center filed a federal lawsuit on behalf of two families who sought to challenge the program. Incredibly, U.S. District Judge Phyllis Hamilton upheld its constitutionality, because it lacked "any devotional or religious intent."[58]

In a baffling departure from the normal aversion to religious matters, the education establishment came out in support of the Islamic curriculum. Tom Meyer, superintendent of the Byron Union School District, praised the judge's decision for leaving teachers free to be creative in addressing matters of religion.[59] Upon appeal, a three-judge panel of the Ninth U.S. Circuit Court of

Appeals issued an unpublished decision affirming Judge Hamilton's decision.

Richard Thompson, chief counsel for Thomas More, criticized the court, noting a blatant double standard that exists in public schools:

> While public schools prohibit Christian students from reading the Bible, praying, displaying the Ten Commandments, and even mentioning the word "God," students in California are being indoctrinated into the religion of Islam. Public schools would never tolerate teaching Christianity in this way. Just imagine the ... outcry if students were told that they had to pray the Lord's Prayer, memorize the Ten Commandments, use such phrases as "Jesus is the Messiah," and fast during Lent.[60]

SEX EDUCATION

Today, public education officials refuse to allow Christian morality to creep into the classroom. After all, they now believe that there are more important matters to discuss, like whether:

- First-graders should be quizzed about "sex feelings in my body."[61]
- School-sponsored magazines should discuss topics like oral sex.[62]
- Students should learn that "it is perfectly natural to be gay."[63]
- Students should learn how to put condoms on cucumbers.[64]
- Taxpayer-funded universities should offer courses on "How to be Gay."[65]

Yet, when national leaders sought to increase funding for "abstinence-only until marriage" programs, the National Education Association opposed their efforts. The NEA claimed that abstinence education "affronts the principle of church-state separation," adding that any message encouraging kids to abstain from sex until marriage "silences speech about sexual orientation."

This wayward learning environment is not without consequences. Reports released by the federal government suggest that students are routinely subjected to far more than immoral sex education lessons. In 2004 the U.S. Department of Education released an in-depth study focusing on sexual misconduct of public school educators. The results were deplorable![66]

One survey, conducted among students in grades 8-11 (ages 13-17), discovered that nearly one out of every ten students (9.6 percent) had experienced "educator sexual misconduct that was unwanted."[67] Another Department of Education study claimed that "more than 4.5 million students are subject to sexual misconduct by an employee of a school sometime between kindergarten and 12th grade."[68]

One study conducted in New York surveyed 225 cases of educator student sexual misconduct in which an educator actually admitted to sexually abusing a student. Researchers were startled to discover that not one of the admitted abusers had been reported to the authorities, and only one percent had lost their license to teach![69] Similar findings were made in other districts.

Sadly, though academic performance in American schools continues to lag behind the rest of the world, many public school proponents opt to use their influence to promote controversial social agendas that have nothing to do with traditional education. While acting as agents of tolerance and diversity, the public schools only fuel America's increasingly bitter culture war.

PUBLIC SCHOOLS: A SOURCE OF CONFLICT

In January 2007, the Cato Institute released a report examining the divisive nature of today's school system. The report, *Why We Fight: How Public Schools Cause Social Conflict*, offers both a clear diagnosis and a commonsense remedy for the contentious nature of public education.

> Rather than bringing people together, public schooling often forces people of disparate backgrounds and beliefs into political combat.... Such clashes are inevitable in government-run schooling because all Americans are required to support the public schools, but only those with the most political power control them....To end the fighting caused by state-run schooling, we should transform our system from one in which government establishes and controls schools, to one in which individual parents are empowered to select schools that share their moral values and educational goals for their children.[70]

Unfortunately, so long as education remains centralized as an established government monopoly, America's children will continue to be force-fed the immoral teachings of secular humanism, and parents who are without financial means will be left with no clear alternative.

PARENTS VS. THE STATE

SAM KASTENSMIDT

The American concept of liberty is unique. Historically, we Americans have looked to God—not government—as the ultimate source of our rights. This philosophy alone can guard the sovereign rights of parents over their children's education and upbringing. However, if America forsakes its religious heritage and yields control to the government, it will have departed from its long heritage of liberty.

Simply put, if our rights do not come from God, then they can be awarded by the government—and taken away just as easily. Indeed, in an atheistic society, no right is inalienable.

Look to the nations which have prided themselves on atheistic frameworks and you will see a vacuum of liberty. In atheistic nations, the government becomes the chief end of man. Consider a resolution adopted in 1918 by the Soviet Union Congress of Educational Workers. It stated,

> We must turn children, who can be shaped like wax, into real good Communists.... We must remove the children from the crude influence of their families. We must take them over and, to speak frankly, nationalize them. From the first days of their lives they will be under the healthy

> influence of Communist children's nurseries and schools. There they will grow up to be real Communists.[1]

America must vigilantly guard against such excesses in the powers of government, particularly in the realm of education, where the minds of future generations are shaped. America is not immune to such abuses of power.

As early as 1922, the state of Oregon passed a law requiring all parents to send their children "to a public school." In response, a concerned Christian academy filed a federal lawsuit, arguing that such a law was "repugnant to the Constitution," because it "conflicts with the right of parents to choose schools where their children will receive appropriate mental and religious training."[2]

On June 1, 1925, in the case of *Pierce v. Society of Sisters*, the U.S. Supreme Court issued a unanimous decision,[3] siding with private schools and affirming the rights of parents.

> We think it entirely plain that the Act of 1922 unreasonably interferes with the liberty of parents and guardians to direct the upbringing and education of children under their control.... The fundamental theory of liberty upon which all governments in this Union repose excludes any general power of the state to standardize its children by forcing them to accept instruction from public teachers only. The child is not the mere creature of the state.[4]

Thankfully, the High Court still recognized the great perils of state-controlled education.

EXPANSIVE GOVERNMENT VS. PARENTAL RIGHTS

Indeed, history has repeatedly shown the dangers of such ambitious plans of government. Only a decade after the Supreme Court reasoned that the "fundamental theory of liberty ... excludes any general power of the state to standardize its children," Adolf Hitler chose another route for the German people, announcing a policy that prohibited parents from privately schooling their children. One of the 25 pillars of Hitler's Nazi Party platform declared, "The *State* is to be responsible for a fundamental reconstruction of our whole national education program."[5]

This experiment—and many others like it—have proven the dangers of state-controlled education. Yet only sixty years after the end of the greatest

World War, a brief look at modern Germany will show that the national government is once again usurping the rights of parents. In a development eerily reminiscent of the fascist era, German officials have actually jailed and levied fines against homeschooling parents who refuse to enroll their children in the nation's schools.[6] In 2006, several children were forcibly removed from their home by police and taken to school.[7]

When Americans voiced concerns to the German Embassy in Chicago, Wolfgang Drautz, Consul General of the Federal Republic of Germany, responded, "The public has a legitimate interest in countering the rise of parallel societies that are based on religion or motivated by different worldviews and in integrating minorities into the population as a whole."[8]

One would assume that such abuses of power would also generate tremendous outrage overseas. Yet, in September 2006, the European Court of Human Rights considered these matters, weighing parental rights against the legitimate powers of government. In a frightening decision, the Court concluded that the State has the right, and perhaps the duty, to seize control of education.

The international court explained,

> Safeguarding pluralism in education … is essential for the preservation of the "democratic society" as conceived by the Convention . . . In view of the power of the modern State, it is above all through *State* teaching that this aim must be realized….Respect is only due to convictions on the part of the parents which do not conflict with the right of the child to education….This means that parents may not refuse the right to education of a child on the basis of their convictions.[9]

AMERICAN COURTS FOLLOW SUIT

Given our long heritage of liberty, most Americans could not conceive of a day when *our* government would likewise strip parents of the basic right to determine the moral content of their child's education. Yet in a modern era plagued by militant secularism and expansive government, it is naïve to assume that America is immune to such egregious rulings. In fact, many determinations of our modern judiciary *already* mirror those of Europe.

In 2001, administrators at the Mesquite Elementary School in Los Angeles' Palmdale School District distributed surveys to elementary school boys and girls—as young as the first grade—asking them how often they had considered "sex feelings in my body," "touching my private parts," and "touching other peoples' private parts." Many parents of these elementary school children were rightly appalled. Several joined in a federal lawsuit against the school district for failing to inform them of the controversial nature of the survey.[10]

On November 2, 2005, the Ninth U.S. Court of Appeals issued a decision explaining that the right "to control the upbringing of their children" was a right that "does not extend beyond the threshold of the school door."[11]

The court declared,

> There is no fundamental right of parents to be the exclusive provider of information regarding sexual matters to their children ... Parents have no due process or privacy right to override the determinations of public schools as to the information to which their children will be exposed while enrolled as students.... Parents ... have no constitutional right ... to prevent a public school from providing its students with whatever information it wishes to provide, sexual or otherwise.[12]

As expected, the parents appealed the ruling to the U.S. Supreme Court, but the High Court declined the appeal—allowing this frightful appellate court decision to stand.[13]

Frankly, it would be quite difficult to explain how this philosophy differs from that of previous fascist regimes—where the government is able to provide children with *"whatever information it wishes to provide,"* and parents *"have no due process or privacy rights to override the determinations of public schools."* Yet this is the current state of public education in America—as federal courts repeatedly assert that parents forfeit the right to be the final arbiter in the education of their children once these little ones reach *"the threshold of the [public] school door."*

In the summer of 2004, a similar case developed when the Boyd County (Ky.) Board of Education announced that all students would be *required* to attend a pro-homosexual "diversity training" seminar. Kevin Theriot, senior legal counsel for the Alliance Defense Fund, reviewed portions of the program and concluded, "It not only puts a gag on students who disagree with homosexual behavior; it also actively attempts to change their moral beliefs."[14]

Hundreds of concerned parents chose to pull their children out of the program. In response, the school board announced that parents had no right to opt their children out of the program, and the district imposed an absolutely mandatory attendance policy. Subsequently, several parents filed a federal lawsuit arguing that the school district had unlawfully stripped them of their fundamental right to determine the moral content of their children's education.

On February 17, 2006, U.S. District Judge David L. Bunning declared that parents' moral and religious convictions would not suffice as an adequate reason to pull their kids out of a seminar. "While parents may have a fundamental right to decide *whether* to send their child to a public school, they do not have a right generally to direct *how* a public school teaches their child," he wrote. "There is simply no basis for an opt-out."[15]

James Esseks, an attorney with the ACLU, concurred, "Parents don't get to say, 'I don't want you to teach evolution or this, that, or whatever else.' If parents don't like it, they can home school; they can go to a private school; they can go to a religious school."[16]

This philosophy runs absolutely counter to America's heritage. As recently as 1969, the U.S. Supreme Court ruled that public schools may not be the sole arbiters of educational content. In a 7-2 decision, the High Court explained,

> In our system, state-operated schools may not be enclaves of totalitarianism... [and] students may not be regarded as closed-circuit recipients of only that which the State chooses to communicate. They may not be confined to the expression of those sentiments that are officially approved.[17]

Yet this is exactly what the state-operated schools are quickly becoming—"enclaves of totalitarianism."

Consider the case of David Parker in Lexington, Massachusetts. On January 14, 2005, his five-year-old son came home from school with a "Diversity Book Bag," which had been given to all *kindergarten* students by the school district. One particular book, *Who's In A Family?*, featured a family headed by a homosexual couple. According to Parker, the book was specifically designed "to indoctrinate young children into the concept that homosexuality and homosexual relationships or marriage are moral and acceptable behavior."[18]

At a meeting with school officials, the Parkers insisted that the elementary school refrain from giving their five-year-old son any materials concerning homosexual relationships, but the school refused. When Mr. Parker peacefully refused to leave the school until the issue was resolved, school officials had him arrested by the Lexington Police Department.

In April 2006, the school failed to provide advance notification to parents before presenting second-graders with *King and King*—a book about homosexual romance and marriage.[19]

The Parkers and two other parents filed a federal lawsuit, contending that the school district had "intruded upon and impaired the adult plaintiffs' clearly established substantive due process rights … as parents and guardians to direct the moral upbringing of their children."[20]

William Hurley, superintendent of the Town of Lexington Public Schools, refused to respect the Parkers' wishes, insisting that the public schools had the right to veto parental sentiments in matters of morality in education. In a motion to dismiss the lawsuit, the school district argued,

> The rights of parents "do not encompass a broad-based right to restrict the flow of information in the public schools." Thus, parents do not have a right "to dictate the curriculum at the public school to which they have chosen to send their children." … [P]arental rights do not end at the schoolhouse door; yet such rights may be limited in the context of a public school.[21]

Not surprisingly, the Massachusetts Teachers Association (MTA) filed an amicus brief, siding with the school district. Incredibly, this teacher union refused to honor parents' wishes. Instead, the union refused to surrender its ability to distribute homosexual romance books and same-sex marriage materials to elementary school children.

> These parents are free to … instruct their children at home about moral and religious matters, to enroll their children in parochial or religious schools, or even to home school their children. What individual parents may not do, however, is demand control over the ideas to which their children will be exposed.[22]

On February 23, 2007, U.S. District Judge Mark L. Wolf issued a 38-paged decision, echoing the arguments of the Massachusetts Teachers Association. The judge explained,

> In essence, under the Constitution, public schools are entitled to teach *anything* that is reasonably related to the goals of preparing students to become engaged and productive citizens in our democracy.... [If they object], the Parkers may send their children to a private school that does not seek to foster understandings of homosexuality or same-sex marriage that conflict with their religious beliefs. They may also educate their children at home.... However, the Parkers ... have chosen to send their children to the Lexington public schools with its current curriculum. The Constitution does not permit them to prescribe what those children will be taught.[23]

While the Parkers have been stripped of the right to determine the moral content of their child's education, they will not be relieved of the obligation to continue to fund these public school messages. As such, modern schools no longer feel any measure of accountability to parents. As the late Nobel Prize winning economist Milton Friedman explained, the public schools "are really not public at all, but simply private fiefs primarily of the administrators and the union officials."[24]

BULLYING PRIVATE CHRISTIAN SCHOOLS

Even private religious schools are now under assault. As Christian parents witness the systematic loss of religious liberty in the nation's public schools, state universities are attempting to impose their secular standards upon private Christian schools.

In 2005, the University of California (UC), which oversees ten separate university campuses, including UCLA and UC-Berkeley, announced that its admissions departments would no longer recognize high school course credits from the Calvary Chapel Christian School (CCCS) in Murrieta, California.[25] Sue Wilbur, director of UC undergraduate admissions, rejected numerous courses, noting that much of the curricula failed to "offer a nonbiased approach."[26]

Wendell Bird, lead attorney for the private school, noted that the state university system had targeted a number of high school courses for presenting a "Christian viewpoint" in subjects like literature, history, and science. Bird pointed out that the University of California, which receives well over $3 billion in annual grants from American taxpayers,[27] challenged course credits from "every major area in high school except for mathematics."

UC officials warned that children educated at the private Christian school "may not be well prepared" for the university level. However, results from a Spring 2005 Stanford Achievement Test showed that students studying under this same curriculum, which is provided by the Association of Christian Schools International (ASCI), outscored students from public schools by 18 to 26 percentile points—depending on the grade and subject matter.[28]

In August 2005, CCCS filed a federal lawsuit against the UC system, claiming that the state had infringed upon the private school's right to convey a religious education. Robert Tyler, the plaintiff's attorney, whose son is enrolled at the school, explained,

> This is America! We have the right to send our kids to private schools, and have them study from a Christian perspective. The [public] university has no right to tell any person of any faith they're not going to accept courses because they are taught from a Christian perspective.... This is all about the culture wars. I think it's pretty obvious; they've chosen sides.[29]

Christopher Patti, counsel for the state university system, responded, "The university is not telling these schools what they can and cannot teach. What the university is doing is simply establishing what is and is not its entrance requirements." Though the state's admissions office rejected these course credits because they were taught from a Christian viewpoint, it is worth noting that the university accepted course credits for public school classes on Islam, "American Pop Culture," "The Jewish Experience," and "Gender, Sexuality, and Identity in Literature."

Wendell Bird, lead attorney for the schools, issued a stern warning about the possible implications if the state is successful in its actions. "This is a liberty case," he explained, "The right of nonpublic institutions to be free. It is very troubling, because it restrains freedom and could spread. Many trends tend to start in California."

If the University of California is successful in closing the door on students from private Christian schools, millions of children—those not attending public schools—could soon forfeit the ability to compete for admission into a state university or community college after high school.

This is yet another consequence of state-controlled education—alongside of academic decline, moral bankruptcy, increased censorship, and an enormous tab for the American taxpayer.

PUBLIC EDUCATION: A SYMPTOM, NOT A CURE

In 1925 (the year of the liberty-affirming *Pierce* decision), the federal budget was less than three billion dollars, and America ran a $700 million surplus.[30] Eighty years later, the nation's budget for public education *alone* dwarfs the entire federal budget of 1925—even after factoring for inflation. In 2005, the American taxpayers spent $536 billion on K-12 schools.[31]

From 1925 to 2006, the comprehensive annual federal budget grew from slightly less than $3 *billion* to just under $3 *trillion*—a marked increase of nearly 1,000-fold in just eighty years.[32] As of 2007, the national debt continues to sprint toward a nearly insurmountable $9 trillion, and our government shows no signs of slowing.

Sadly, as the government grows in size and power, the great institutions that once laid the foundations for American liberty—the Church and the family—have incrementally yielded control to the State. Never sated, the appetite of government for power and funding will only swell. Tremendous debts that will require "draconian" solutions await our children and grandchildren.

This is not a fringe position; it is a sentiment of Federal Reserve Chairman Ben Bernanke. In January 2007, he testified before Congress about the looming fiscal crisis that is fast approaching unless America gains control of government spending:

> We are experiencing what seems likely to be the calm before the storm.... However, if early and meaningful action is not taken, the U.S. economy could be seriously weakened, with future generations bearing much of the cost.... The longer we wait, the more severe, the more draconian, the more difficult the adjustments are going to be.[33]

If Americans want to spare future generations from the consequences of a failing educational system, abandonment of moral standards, and the reckless encroachment of expansive government, then parents and the Church must reclaim the roles they once held in our nation—those to which Scripture calls them! As Christians, we have a covenantal obligation to ensure that future generations are not forced to pay for our failure to act.

THE GROWTH OF GOVERNMENT & THE LOSS OF LIBERTY

It has long been said, "That government is best which governs least."

Almost invariably, experience has proven this axiom true. History has shown that bloated government leads to the loss of individual liberty. Today, far too many Americans mistakenly look to the government—not God—as the ultimate arbiter of rights. In doing so, they forsake a rich heritage which was founded upon the belief that all men "are endowed by their Creator with certain unalienable rights."

Sen. Barry Goldwater was absolutely right when he warned, "A government that is big enough to give you all you want is big enough to take it all away." Though our expansive government has proven itself ineffective, Americans continue to feed this clumsy giant—clinging to some starved hope that a distant bureaucracy will somehow solve the nation's troubles. As we do so, we only assist in the exchange of liberty for shackles.

James Madison warned against the expansion of government, noting that tyranny does not typically emerge overnight. "There are more instances of the abridgement of the freedom of the people by the gradual and silent encroachment of those in power than by violent and sudden usurpation."

In the last century it was a gradual process in which parents yielded their responsibilities to the public schools. Today, if we are to stave off this silent encroachment, the sheer enormity and ineffectiveness of our failed public education system must be addressed.

ALTERNATIVES THAT WORK

DR. GARY CASS AND SAM KASTENSMIDT

Bloated and never sated in its quest for more funds and power, America's increasingly centralized public education system has led to sharply lower academic and moral standards and a severe erosion of parental authority.

This problem has for decades been recognized by many of our nation's leaders. In 1982, during his first State of the Union address, President Ronald Reagan called for "dismantling the Department of Education." One year later, after examining the Department of Education's own report on the failing nature of the public schools, President Reagan delivered a radio address to the nation, admitting a crisis in America's public schools. He stated,

> The quality of learning in our classrooms has been declining for the last two decades ... years when the Federal presence in education grew and grew. Parental control over local schools shrank. Bureaucracy ballooned until accountability seemed lost. Parents were frustrated and didn't know where to turn.[1]

In an effort to return control to parents and local school boards, many politicians have sought to downsize the federal government's role in education.

In 1995, inspired by the leadership of Reagan, U.S. Congressman Joe Scarborough once again sought to dismantle the Department of Education. His legislation explained that this was necessary "to return the responsibility and authority for education to parents, teachers, communities, students, and States," as well as "to ensure that the Federal Government does not overregulate and interfere in the decision-making of parents..." Though his bill gained 120 co-sponsors, it was never allowed an up or down vote on the House floor.

EMERGING TRENDS

Given the academic and moral failure of the public school system, many parents and public officials are now giving serious consideration to new alternatives for educating the nation's children, including charter schools, homeschooling, private Christian schools, school voucher programs, and tuition tax credits.

Each of these alternatives has made substantial progress in recent years—offering encouraging signs that education is being spared from the clutches of government. The number of homeschooled students has grown exponentially in the past few decades—from roughly twelve thousand students in 1978 to more than 1.7 million students in 2000.[2] Between 1990 and 2001, the enrollment of students in private schools jumped by 500,000 students.[3] Both federal and state legislatures are now debating the merits of school voucher programs and tuition tax credits, which the Supreme Court has already declared to be constitutional.

PUBLIC CHARTER SCHOOLS

The Charter School movement is an attempt to reform public education. In order to encourage innovation, charter schools—while still very much under the control of the government—are freed from much of the onerous red tape and complicated codes that burden public schools. Nevertheless, they still employ a secular humanistic curriculum.

Studies have shown that charter schools are more academically effective than public schools. This was examined by Harvard economist Caroline Hoxby. In a 2004 study, she reported,

> Compared to students in the matched public school, charter students are 5.2 percent more likely to be proficient in reading and 3.2 percent more likely to be proficient in math on their state's exams. Charter schools that have been in

> operation longer have a greater proficiency advantage over the matched public schools.[4]

HOMESCHOOLING

In his book, *Bridging Liberalism and Multiculturalism in American Education*, Rob Reich, a professor of political science at Stanford University, noted,

> Homeschooling is no longer a fringe phenomenon in American education.... [The number of homeschooled students] is greater than the combined number of students enrolled in schools in Wyoming, Alaska, Delaware, North Dakota, Vermont, South Dakota, Montana, Rhode Island, New Hampshire, and Hawaii..."[5]

Indeed, the homeschooling movement has spread like wildfire throughout America—and with good reason. Not only are parents able to direct their child's moral upbringing, but the average homeschooled student, quite simply, dominates the competition. In its report, "The Scholastic Achievement of Homeschool Students," the Education Resources Information Center explained,

> Home school student achievement test scores were exceptionally high.... On average, home school students in grades 1 to 4 performed one grade level above their age-level public/private school peers on achievement tests. Students who had been home schooled their entire academic life had higher scholastic achievement test scores than students who had also attended other educational programs.... Almost 25% of home school students were enrolled one or more grades above their age-level peers in public and private schools.[6]

The study also noted, "On standardized achievement tests, the homeschooled students performed at or above the 80th percentile on national norms in reading, listening, language, math, science, social studies, basic battery, and complete battery scores."[7] The study concludes, "[P]arents choosing to make a commitment to home schooling were able to provide a very successful academic environment."

Not surprisingly, the most fundamentally Christian model for education—

children learning directly from their parents (as described in Deuteronomy 6)—produces the best results.

TITHING SCHOOLS

There is also a growing number of the lesser known "Tithing Schools," designed to help make Christian education accessible to families who tithe to their local church and commit to regularly volunteer in the school. This method of schooling is a great help to young families who not only tithe to their local church, but also labor to pay private school tuition.

This practice is not without biblical precedence. The Old Testament Levites were supported by the tithe and were responsible both for cultivating the worship and education of the people of God. This method also strengthens the bonds within the sponsoring church—by bringing families together for more than just Sunday morning worship.

Indeed, most Christians would be delighted to see their church filled with children receiving Christian instruction during the week. They would be excited to participate in such a worthy cause. This may be just the kind of urgent reprioritizing that is needed to take back our children from the clutches of a secular education.

CLASSICAL CHRISTIAN EDUCATION

A revival in classical education is also beginning to sweep across the nation. The Association of Classical Christian Schools now has 185 member schools educating approximately 40,000 students. In addition, an estimated 50,000 homeschooled students are using some form of classical Christian curriculum in their studies.[8]

Classical education constitutes a return to the teaching methods used before and during our founding era. Classical education is based on the style of instruction that was employed in the famous Boston Latin Grammar School. It is the approach that had been refined over centuries of Western Civilization—only to be discarded under the influences of modern educational theories.

Nevertheless, Western Civilization owes a great deal to classical education and its use of the ancient Trivium—grammar, logic, and rhetoric. This educational theory "cuts with the grain," taking advantage of a child's natural learning process. Children exposed to this way of learning experience an exciting, yet rigorous, education.

Parents must use caution when choosing any school for their children.

Not all classical programs or Christian academies are committed to a scriptural worldview, nor are they each doctrinally sound. Parents must inspect the school's doctrinal standards and enrollment policies before enrolling their child.

PRIVATE SCHOOLS

There are over six million children[9] enrolled in America's nearly 30,000 private schools.[10] According to the Department of Education's own studies, private religious schools significantly outperform public schools.

In its report, "Student Achievement in Private Schools," the National Assessment of Education Progress declared,

> Students at grades 4, 8, and 12 in all categories of private schools had higher average scores in reading, mathematics, science, and writing than their counterparts in public schools. In addition, higher percentages of students in private schools performed at or above *Proficient* compared to those in public schools.[11]

The report continued, "For each assessment discussed in this report at each grade, students as a whole in every category of private schools had a higher average score than their counterparts in public schools."[12] The government's own reports admit that private schools outperform the public schools in "every category."

PARENTAL CHOICE (SCHOOL VOUCHERS)

If the government's own studies now show that private education has fared far better than public education, one must wonder why so many continue to support the centralized $536 billion public education industry, which vigorously opposes any measure that might break the government's monopoly and allow for more parental control in matters of education.

School vouchers provide parents with the option of sending their children to private schools with tax-funded vouchers to help defer the cost of tuition. As of 2007, approximately 150,000 students participate in publicly funded tuition scholarship programs,[13] and this number is expected to grow considerably in the coming years.

Some proponents of vouchers (or "school choice") programs contend that competition between the public and private sectors will ultimately benefit education in general—leading to greater efficiency and better academic results for both public and private schools.

Other proponents believe school vouchers are necessary to ensure educational equality. Ted Sizer, professor of education at Harvard University, explains, "The issue [is whether] all families have the same choice that upper and middle class Americans have, or should the system remain as it is, giving mobility to those who could buy it and leaving the rest as they are."[14] These arguments appeal to a sense of fairness. All parents, rich or poor, who send their kids to private schools are forced to pay twice—taxes for the public school they are not utilizing and tuition for the private school.

Teacher unions oppose vouchers, arguing that all parents who send their children to private schools should be forced to pay twice in order to prevent the diversion of funds from public schools. They contend that such practices only wound an already ailing educational system.

Yet Harvard University economist Caroline Hoxby has shown that vouchers ultimately aid both private and public systems. In a study examining the impact of voucher programs on public schools, Hoxby discovered that the public schools facing the most direct competition from private schools showed the greatest improvements in academic performance—and vice-versa.[15]

A report released by the Heritage Foundation declared,

> In addition to helping participating children, school choice programs introduce competition into public school systems, which can drive public schools to improve performance or risk losing students. Studies have suggested that competition has a desirable system-wide effect, encouraging traditional public schools threatened with a loss of students to make better use of their resources.[16]

Yet some Christian scholars are hesitant to embrace voucher programs. In a 2002 article, Marshall Fritz, founder of the Alliance for the Separation of School and State, presented four arguments against vouchers.[17]

- First, vouchers come with strings attached, allowing government bureaucracy to become a chief source of funding for private schools, making increased government influence inevitable.
- Second, vouchers could foster a sense of government dependency among families who would otherwise pay for

private schooling on their own.

- Third, government vouchers could eventually be conditioned upon a requirement that private schools consent to nondiscrimination clauses—pressuring these private schools to admit students who reject the school's stated beliefs or code of conduct.
- Finally, vouchers could be counter-productive in fostering private enterprise. By introducing government aid to private schools, administrators are likely to become increasingly complacent and less innovative in providing quality education at low costs.

Regardless of the potential pitfalls, research has shown that these programs tend to improve education for all students.

The Cleveland Scholarship Program (CSP), one of the first voucher programs in the nation, was adopted in hopes of remedying the disastrous condition of public schools in Cleveland's inner city. Researchers from Harvard, Stanford, and the University of Texas closely monitored this program. In June 1999, Harvard's Kennedy School of Government sponsored a report, "An Evaluation of the Cleveland Voucher Program After Two Years."

The report's findings noted that "nearly half of the parents in choice schools reported being 'very satisfied' with the academic program of their child's school, as compared to less than 30 percent of public school parents.... The differences in satisfaction rates were also large when parents were asked about the teachers' skills, the teaching of moral values, and class size."[18]

In addition to parental satisfaction, the academic performance of these students showed marked improvement over their public school counterparts. The report continued,

> Test score results in mathematics and reading show substantial gains for CSP students ... Between the fall of 1996 and the spring of 1998, these students, on average, gained relative to the national norm 7 percentile points on the reading test and 15 percentile points in math.[19]

Sadly, just one month after this encouraging report was published, a federal lawsuit was filed aimed at striking down Ohio's "school choice" program. The plaintiffs claimed that because many students used school vouchers to attend religious schools, the program constituted an unlawful government endorsement of religious schools. Ignoring the verifiable successes of the voucher program, secularist organizations, including the National Education Association and the American Civil Liberties Union vehemently opposed the program—fearing that the government's monopolistic control of education might be splintered.

Dr. D. James Kennedy, president and founder of Coral Ridge Ministries, pointed out the blatant double standard of these organizations:

> [The discussion of school vouchers] introduces two things: it introduces the element of choice, and it introduces the element of free enterprise and competition, both of which are supposedly American virtues today. Yet the people who are so vociferous when it comes to choice in things like abortion … are the people most adamantly opposed to this system of choice in education.[20]

Thankfully, on June 27, 2002, the U.S. Supreme Court upheld the parents' "right to choose," issuing a sharply divided 5-4 decision. This decision affirmed the constitutionality of Ohio's school voucher programs. Chief Justice William Rehnquist authored the Court's opinion:

> We have repeatedly recognized that no reasonable observer would think a neutral program of private choice, where state aid reaches religious schools solely as a result of the numerous independent decisions of private individuals, carries with it the *imprimatur* of government endorsement.… It is part of a general and multifaceted undertaking by the State of Ohio to provide educational opportunities to the children of a failed school district.[21]

Though the U.S. Supreme Court affirmed the constitutionality of school vouchers, numerous other courts have concluded that school choice programs violate their respective state constitutions. In particular, courts have ruled that the programs violated Blaine amendments—a series of anti-Catholic constitutional amendments passed by 37 states in the late nineteenth century. These amendments forbade the states from providing public aid to private or religious institutions.

In making such rulings, these state and federal courts opted to ignore the Supreme Court's affirmation of the voucher programs—namely that voucher programs merely provide parents with the ability to make their own private choices regarding private education. In so doing, these courts essentially sentenced low-income children to a lifetime of government schooling.

Nevertheless, parents and lawmakers are seeing the proven track record of "school choice" programs, and the push for these programs is gaining momentum. In 2006, 29 state legislatures debated private school vouchers—with seven states enacting measures to promote them.[22]

PRIVATE SCHOOL TAX CREDITS

Another method of increasing parental control in education comes in the form of private school tuition tax credits. These programs offer the same upsides of vouchers without inviting government involvement into the affairs of private schools. By using tuition tax credits, parents would be able to reduce their annual tax burden by applying a portion of their annual private school tuition expenses toward the tax bill. This program addresses the unfairness of forcing parents with children in private schools to pay twice—funding both public schools with taxes and private schools with tuition.

For example, under a system of tuition tax credits, parents who spent $5,000 for private school tuition would be permitted to reduce their annual tax liability by $5,000—depending on the caps set by the state or federal governments.

An increasingly popular style of this reform was started in Arizona, where *all* taxpayers are invited to reduce their annual tax burden by making voluntary donations (up to $500) to "school tuition organizations" (STOs), which then distribute the funds to families seeking to send their children to private schools.

Under Arizona's dollar-for-dollar tax credit, any taxpayer who contributes $500 to these private school scholarship funds can then reduce their own state tax liability by $500. It becomes a choice for the taxpayers. They are given a choice: funding either private schools or the government.

Already, the program has proven tremendously successful. Most Americans realize that the private sector is far more efficient than government bureaucracy. In 2000, tens of thousands of Arizona taxpayers participated in the state's tax credit program, generating private scholarships for 15,000 students. The Cato Institute estimates that nearly 37,000 families with children in private schools will directly benefit from these tax credits by 2015.[23]

This style of educational reform is gaining momentum throughout the nation. Tuition tax credit programs now exist in Arizona, Florida, Illinois, Iowa, Pennsylvania, and Minnesota—with a number of states seriously debating similar legislation.[24] A similar measure has also been debated in the U.S. House.

David Salisbury, director of the Center for Educational Freedom, believes that this momentum may ultimately provide a way for parents to reassert themselves in the education of youth. Salisbury argued,

> [I]n a political climate driven by enthusiasm for national standards, a carefully crafted federal tax credit may help neutralize Washington's role in what should be a state matter. While the [federal] tax credit will not revolutionize education, it may motivate states to take similar actions, expanding educational freedom for parents and children. The emergence of the ... bill in Congress shows an increasing agreement that it is permissible to empower parents to choose the schools their children attend. Now states need to pick up the ball and begin to lead, as they should, on the issue of school choice.[25]

THE EXODUS MANDATE

While proponents of the status quo are quick to denigrate these alternatives to public schools, one thing stands undeniably true. Each of these alternatives has produced better results than the current system of public education.

Consequently, the deterioration of the public school system and the increased availability of viable alternatives have led major Christian denominations to debate whether Christian parents should withdraw their children from the public schools. At the 2006 Southern Baptist Convention, Roger Moran and Dr. Bruce N. Shortt introduced a proposal calling upon the denomination to develop an "exit strategy from the public schools."

One proponent of the measure was Dr. R. Albert Mohler, Jr., president of the prominent Southern Baptist Theological Seminary in Louisville, Kentucky. He explained,

> I believe that now is the time for responsible Southern Baptists to develop an exit strategy from the public schools. This strategy would affirm the basic and ultimate responsibility of Christian parents to take charge of the education of

> their own children. The strategy would also affirm the responsibility of churches to equip parents, support families, and offer alternatives.[26]

Likewise, the Presbyterian Church in America (PCA) debated a resolution which sought to encourage parents to "remove their children from public schools and see to it that they receive a thoroughly Christian education."[27]

The resolution, which had the support of Dr. Kennedy, was sponsored by Pastor Steven Warhurst, who explained, "We are people who drank heavily from the trough of state education and realized that it's poisonous. And now we have found cisterns of living water, so to speak—and we would love other people to join us. I would love to see every family in the Presbyterian Church in America take their children out of the public schools. . . ."[28]

Though both of these resolutions ultimately failed, the fact that they were seriously considered in two of the nation's leading conservative evangelical denominations highlights the growing tension between the nation's public schools and Christian values. Sadly, there are no encouraging signs of reform from within the public schools.

As Dr. Mohler observed, "With control over the public school system increasingly in the hands of the courts, educational bureaucrats, the university-based education schools, and the powerful teachers' unions, little hope for correction appears."[29]

Decades ago, President Reagan warned the nation about the dangers of permitting the government to strip education out of the homes. His philosophy, which recognized that the "government does not solve problems; it subsidizes them," has been validated. Sadly, the national problems in public education which plagued Reagan's era have only grown worse with time. In 1983, Reagan remarked,

> [G]overnment seemed to forget that education begins in the home, where it's a parental right and responsibility. Both our private and our public schools exist to aid your families in the instruction of your children. For too many years, people here in Washington acted like your families' wishes were only getting in the way. We've seen what that "Washington knows best" attitude has wrought. Our high standards of literacy and educational diversity have been slipping. Well-intentioned but misguided policymakers have stamped a

> uniform mediocrity on the rich variety and excellence that had been our heritage. I think most parents agree it's time to change course. We must move education forward again, with common sense as our guide. We must put the basics back in the schools and the parents back in charge.[30]

When Americans considered education to be a family matter, in cooperation with the Church, schooling was not heavily subsidized or controlled by the government, yet our literacy rates and academic standards were the envy of the world. Decentralized and free, education in America thrived. Yet in recent decades, churches and families have yielded the responsibility of education to a government that is increasingly hostile to the core tenets of Christianity, and we have seen the disastrous results.

"Parents must not allow their children to be taught an atheistic view of the world if they have any choice in the matter," stated Dr. Kennedy. "Parents have the God-given responsibility to provide the best Christian education they can for their children, given their circumstances, finances, and teaching abilities. This responsibility to train up children in the way they should go is the most important and sacred trust given to a Christian couple (Proverbs 22:6)."

Now more than ever, it is imperative for Christian parents to make a stand for their families.

ENDNOTES

INTRODUCTION

1 Acts 10:36
2 Acts 20:26-27

THE BIBLE AND EDUCATION

1 John 8:32
2 John 8:31-32
3 John 18:37
4 1 Corinthians 1:20, 25
5 Mark 12:29-31
6 Psalm 90:12, KJV.
7 2 Corinthians 10:5
8 Psalm 147:5
9 Charles Hodge, *Systematic Theology*, (Eerdmans, Grand Rapids, 1986) Vol. 1, p. 396.
10 Hebrews 4:13; Psalm 94:9; Psalm 139:1-2; Proverbs 15:3, 11; Ezekiel 11:5; Acts 15:18; Matthew 10:30.
11 1 John 3:20
12 1 Corinthians 1:20
13 1 Corinthians 6:19
14 John 1:1
15 Colossians 2:2-3
16 1 Corinthians 2:14
17 Romans 12:1-2
18 "Protagorus," Internet Encyclopedia of Philosophy. http://www.iep.utm.edu/p/protagor.htm
19 Genesis 3:5
20 Clark, Gordon H., *A Christian Philosophy of Education* (Eerdmans, Grand Rapids, 1946) p.27.
21 John 14:6
22 Psalm 36:1-4
23 Proverbs 1:7
24 *Matthew Henry's Commentary on the Whole Bible: New Modern Edition*, Electronic Database. Copyright (c) 1991 by Hendrickson Publishers, Inc.
25 Luke 17:2
26 Ephesians 6:4
27 Deuteronomy 6:6-9
28 Leviticus 10:11

THE FOUNDERS AND EDUCATION

1 Adam Cohen, "According to Webster: One Man's Attempt to Define 'America,'" *The New York Times*, February 12, 2006. http://nytimes.com/2006/02/12/opinion/12sun3.html?ex=1297400400&en=48fd62e8bf2712ca&ei=5090
2 "Noah Webster," *Wikipedia*, January 30, 2007. http://en.wikipedia.org/wiki/Noah_Webster
3 Mark M. Alexander, "Expelling God From the Academy," Townhall.com, December 8, 2006. http://www.townhall.com/columnists/MarkMAlexander/2006/12/08/expelling_god_from_the_academy
4 Ibid.
5 "The First New Hampshire Teacher: John Legat," Museum of New Hampshire History, 2004. http://nhhistory.org/edu/support/nhgrowingup/firstnhteacher.pdf
6 Ibid.
7 "The True-Blue Laws of Connecticut and New Haven," Edited by J. Hammond Trumbull, 1876. http://www.quinnipiac.edu/other/abl/etext/trueblue/bluelaws.html
8 David Barton, *Original Intent*, WallBuilder Press, Aledo, Texas, 2000, p. 81.
9 *The Literatures of Colonial America: An Anthology*, Edited by Susan Castillo and Ivy Schweitzer,

Blackwell Publishers, Malden, Massachusetts, 2001.
10 David Limbaugh, *Persecution: How Liberals Are Waging War Against Christianity*, Harper Collins, New York, 2004.
11 Don Closson, "Student Rights," Probe Ministries, 1995. http://www.leaderu.com/orgs/probe/docs/st-rts.html
12 William J. Federer, *America's God and Country*, Amerisearch, Inc., St. Louis, Missouri, 2000.
13 Ibid.
14 Randy McNutt, "Oxford Pays Tribute to 'McGuffey Reader' Writer," *The Cincinnati Enquirer*, September 21, 2000. http://www.enquirer.com/editions/2000/09/21/loc_oxford_pays_tribute.html
15 "William Holmes McGuffey and His Readers," *The Museum Gazette*, U.S. Department of Interior: The National Park Service, January 1993. http://www.nps.gov/jeff/historyculture/upload/mcguffey.pdf
16 David Barton, *Original Intent*, WallBuilder Press, Aledo, Texas, 2000, p. 81.
17 Ibid, p. 82.
18 Ibid.
19 Ibid, p. 84.
20 Ibid.
21 William J. Federer, *America's God and Country*, FAME Publishing, Coppell, Texas, 1994, p. 520.
22 Ibid., p. 704.
23 "Milestones: A Short History of Princeton University," *Princeton University Handbook*, June 2005. http://www.princeton.edu/hr/handbook/history.htm
24 Steven T. Voigt, *Tyranny: The Collapse of Traditional Law in America*, Infinity Publishing, Haverford, Pennsylvania, 2004.
25 David Barton, "God: Missing in Action from American History," WallBuilders, June 2005. http://www.wallbuilders.com/resources/search/detail.php?ResourceID=121
26 Thucydides (c. 460–400 B.C.), Athenian historian. Quoted by Dionysius of Halicarnassus in Ars Rhetorica, ch. 11, sect. 2.
27 *Ethics Newsline*, Volume 5, Number 25, Institute for Global Ethics, June 24, 2002.
28 Augustine on *Christian Doctrine*, Book II, Chapter 40, par. 60.
29 James Madison, A Letter to W.T. Barry, 1822. http://press-pubs.uchicago.edu/founders/documents/v1ch18s35.html
30 Noah Webster, "On the Education of Youth in America," 1788.
31 *The Federalist Papers*, edited by Isaac Kramnick, Penguin Books, London, England, 1987, p. 29.
32 Plato, *The Republic*, Book VIII, trans. Allan Bloom, New York: Basic Books, 1968.
33 Kramnick, , p. 319.
34 Kramnick, , p. 13.
35 Peter Lillback with Jerry Newcombe, *George Washington's Sacred Fire*, "The Christian Education of George Washington," Providence Forum Press, Bryn Mawr, Pennsylvania, 2006, p. 111.
36 George Washington, Farewell Address, September 17, 1796.
37 Joseph Farah, "Is God bad for society?," *WorldNetDaily*, September 29, 2005. http://www.worldnetdaily.com/news/article.asp?ARTICLE_ID=46575
38 Benjamin Franklin, *The Papers of Benjamin Franklin*, "Proposals Relating to the Education of Youth in Pennsylvania," 1749, Leonard W. Labaree (Ed.), Yale University Press, New Haven, volume III, p. 413, 1961.
39 Barton, *Original Intent*, p. 153.
40 The Northwest Ordinance, 1787. http://usinfo.state.gov/usa/infousa/facts/democrac/5.htm
41 *Vidal v. Girard's Executors*, Supreme Court of the United States, 1844.
42 "Religion and the Founding of the American Republic," The Library of Congress, 2007. http://www.loc.gov/exhibits/religion/rel04.html
43 Benjamin Rush, "Of the Mode of Education Proper in a Republic," 1798. http://press-pubs.uchicago.edu/founders/documents/v1ch18s30.html
44 Federer, p. 247.

FROM THE FOUNDERS TO DEWEY: THE ROLE OF IDEAS

1 Alexis de Tocqueville, *Democracy in America*, Book I, Chapter 8, 1831. http://xroads.virginia.edu/~HYPER/DETOC/1_ch08.htm
2 The Declaration of Independence.
3 "The Other Side of 1984," Lesslie Newbigin, p. 7, The Risk Book Series 1983.
4 *Wikipedia*, Immanuel Kant, http://en.wikipedia.org/wiki/Kant
5 Kant's Philosophy of Religion, *Stanford Encyclopedia of Philosophy*, http://plato.stanford.edu/entries/kant-religion/#3.9

6 Immanuel Kant, "An Answer to the Question: What is Enlightenment?" September 30, 1784.
7 Westminster Shorter Catechism, no.2.
8 Romans 1:19
9 George Washington, Farewell Address, 1796. http://usinfo.state.gov/usa/infousa/facts/democrac/49.htm
10 Edward Younkins, "Rousseau's General Will and Well Ordered Society," Le Quebecois Libre, no.156. http://www.quebecoislibre.org/05/050715-16.htm
11 Ibid.
12 Pierre Nora, "Rethinking the French Past of Memory," Columbia University Press, New York, 1996, p. 150.
13 Younkins, no. 156.
14 Gordon H. Clark, *William James and John Dewey*, The Trinity Foundation, pp. 5-6.
15 Carl Mickelsen, "Hegel Glossary," University of Idaho, 2007. http://www.class.uidaho.edu/mickelsen/texts/Hegel%20Glossary.htm
16 G. K. Chesterton, *Orthodoxy*, Chapter 3: "The Suicide of Thought," 1908.
17 Mel and Norma Gabler, *What Are They Teaching Our Children*, Victor Books, 1985., p.25.
18 "Only a Teacher—Schoolhouse Pioneers," PBS, http://www.pbs.org/onlyateacher/horace.html
19 Ibid.
20 "Horace Mann," Encarta Encyclopedia, 2007. http://encarta.msn.com/encnet/refpages/RefMedia.aspx?refid=461530354&artrefid=1741500823&sec=-1&pn=1
21 Alexis de Tocqueville, *Democracy in America*, Book II, Chapter 8, 1840.
22 Mark M. Alexander, "Expelling God From the Academy," Townhall.com, December 8, 2006. http://www.townhall.com/columnists/MarkMAlexander/2006/12/08/expelling_god_from_the_academy
23 Clark, p. 7.
24 William James quoted in Clark , p. 25.
25 Ibid.
26 "Teachers Meet," *Time Magazine*, July 11, 1932. http://www.time.com/time/magazine/article/0,9171,743991-2,00.html
27 Gabler, pp. 26.
28 *Humanist Manifesto I*, American Humanist Association, 1933. http://www.americanhumanist.org/about/manifesto1.html
29 *Humanist Manifesto I*, American Humanist Association, 1933. http://www.americanhumanist.org/about/manifesto1.html
30 Gabler, pp. 29.
31 *Wikipedia* at http://en.wikipedia.org/wiki/Black_Book_of_Communism
32 Dr. John Dewey, *My Pedagogic Creed*, E. L. Kellogg & Company, 1897.
33 *Articles of Faith, Articles of Peace: Religious Liberty Clauses and the American Public Philosophy*, James Davison Hunter and Os Guinness: editors, Brookings Institution Press, 1990, p.70.
34 *Torcaso v. Watkins*, 367 U.S. 488 Supreme Court of the United States, June 19, 1961.
35 John Dunphy, "A Religion of a New Age," *The Humanist*, January/February 1983, p. 26.
36 *Engel v. Vitale*, *Thompson Gale Legal Encyclopedia*, Answers.com, 2006. http://www.answers.com/topic/engel-v-vitale
37 *Abington v. Schempp*, 1963.
38 *Epperson v. Arkansas*, 1968.
39 *Stone v. Graham*, 1980.
40 *Wallace v. Jaffree*, 1985.
41 *Edwards v. Aguillard*, 1987.
42 *Allegheny v. ACLU*, 1989.
43 *Lee v. Weisman*, 1992.
44 *Locke v. Davey*, 2003.
45 Dr. John Dewey, *My Pedagogic Creed*, E. L. Kellogg & Company, 1897.

MEASURING THE DECLINE

1 "Horace Mann," *Encarta Encyclopedia*, 2007.http://encarta.msn.com/encnet/refpages/RefMedia.aspx?refid=461530354&artrefid=1741500823&sec=-1&pn=1
2 National Commission on Excellence in Education, *A Nation at Risk*, April 1983. http://www.ed.gov/pubs/NatAtRisk/risk.html
3 President Ronald Reagan, "Remarks on Receiving the Final Report of the National Commission on Excellence in Education," University of Texas Archives, April 26, 1983. http://www.reagan.utexas.edu/archives/speeches/1983/42683d.htm

4 Charles J. Sykes, *Dumbing Down Our Kids*, St. Martin's Press, New York, New York, 1995.
5 Robert Holland and Don Soifer, "Waste in Public Schools Produce Low Literacy Return for the Dollars Spent," The Friedman Foundation, June 1, 2000. http://www.friedmanfoundation.org/news/2000-06-01.html
6 Lori Aratani, "Upper Grades, Lower Reading Skills," *The Washington Post*, July 13, 2006. http://www.washingtonpost.com/wp-dyn/content/article/2006/07/12/AR2006071201825.html
7 Lois Romano, "Literacy of College Graduates Is on Decline," *The Washington Post*, December 25, 2005. http://www.washingtonpost.com/wp-dyn/content/article/2005/12/24/AR2005122400701.html
8 Garrick Davis, "Literary Reading in Dramatic Decline, According to National Endowment for the Arts Survey," National Endowment for the Arts News Room, July 8, 2004. http://www.nea.gov/news/news04/ReadingAtRisk.html
9 "Reading at Risk: A Survey of Literary Reading in America," National Endowment for the Arts, June 2004. http://www.nea.gov/pub/ReadingAtRisk.pdf
10 Jeff Jacoby, "The Ignorant American Voter," *The Boston Globe*, October 24, 2004. http://www.boston.com/news/globe/editorial_opinion/oped/articles/2004/10/24/the_ignorant_american_voter/
11 Noah Webster, "On the Education of Youth in America," 1788.
12 "Final Report: National Geographic-Roper Public Affairs 2006 Geographic Literacy Study," The National Geographic Education Foundation, May 2006, p. 6. http://www.nationalgeographic.com/roper2006/pdf/FINALReport2006GeogLitsurvey.pdf
13 "Final Report" p. 7.
14 "Education at a Glance: OECD Indicators 2005," Organisation for Economic Cooperation and Development, 2005. http://www.oecd.org/dataoecd/20/25/35345692.pdf
15 "The 2004 Brown Center Report on American Education: How Well Are American Students Learning," Brookings Institution: Brown Center on Educational Policy, November 2004. http://www.brookings.org/gs/brown/bc_report/2004/2004report.pdf
16 "2000 National Survey of Science and Mathematics Education," Horizon Research Incorporated, December 2002, p. 6. http://2000survey.horizon-research.com/reports/mid_math/mid_math.pdf
17 Brit Hume, "Zogby Poll: Most Americans Can Name Three Stooges, But Not Three Branches of Gov't," *FOX News*, August 15, 2006.
18 "The Coming Crisis in Citizenship: Higher Education's Failure to Teach America's History and Institutions," Intercollegiate Studies Institute: American Civic Literacy Program, September 26, 2006. http://www.americancivicliteracy.org/report/pdf/09-26-06/civic_literacy_report.pdf
19 "The Coming Crisis, 2006.
20 "Building A 21st Century Workforce," U.S. Department of Energy: Office of Science, 2007. http://www.er.doe.gov/Sub/Occasional_Papers/2-Occ-21st-Century-Workforce.PDF
21 David Crary, "Study: College Students More Narcissistic," Associated Press, February 27, 2007. http://apnews.myway.com/article/20070227/D8NHS51O0.html
22 Paul Ciotti, "America's Most Costly Educational Failure," Cato Institute, April 29, 1998. http://www.cato.org/dailys/4-29-98.html
23 Ibid.
24 "Kansas City School District Loses Accreditation," CNN, May 3, 2000. http://cnnstudentnews.cnn.com/2000/fyi/teacher.resources/education.news/05/03/kansas.city/index.html
25 "Projections of Education Statistics to 2012," Thirty-First Edition, National Center for Education Statistics, October 2002, p. 12. http://nces.ed.gov/pubs2002/2002030.pdf
26 "10 Facts About K-12 Education Funding," U.S. Department of Education, June 2005. http://www.ed.gov/about/overview/fed/10facts/10facts.pdf
27 "Why Should Congress Abolish the Federal Role in Education?" National Center for Home Education, January 12, 2000. http://www.hslda.org/docs/nche/000000/00000063.asp
28 "SAT Score Averages of College-Bound Seniors," National Center for Education Statistics, Digest of *Education Statistics*, 2004. http://nces.ed.gov/programs/digest/d04/tables/dt04_129.asp
29 "Statistics About Non-Public Education in the United States," U.S. Department of Education, 2004. http://www.ed.gov/about/offices/list/oii/nonpublic/statistics.html
30 D. James Kennedy, Ph.D., *Education: Public Problems & Private Solutions*, Coral Ridge Ministries, Fort Lauderdale, Fla., p. 49.
31 "National Assessment of Educational Progress: Comparing Private Schools and Public Schools Using Hierarchical Linear Modeling," U.S. Department of Education: National Center for Education Statistics, July 2006. http://nces.ed.gov/nationsreportcard/pdf/studies/2006461.pdf
32 "Check the Facts: The NCES Private-Public School Study," The Hoover Institution, Winter 2007. http://media.hoover.org/documents/ednext_20071_75.pdf
33 John Stossel, "Stupid in America: How We Cheat Our Kids," *ABC News*, January 13, 2006. http://abcnews.go.com/2020/Stossel/story?id=1500338
34 Deborah Kolben, "Stossel Talks to Teachers Protesting ABC's 'Stupid in America' Segment," *The New York Sun*, March 9, 2006. http://www.nysun.com/article/28849

35 D. James Kennedy, Ph.D., p. 4-5, 10.
36 Milton Friedman, "Public Schools: Make Them Private," The Cato Institute, June 23, 1995. http://www.cato.org/pubs/briefs/bp-023.html
37 D. James Kennedy, Ph.D., p. 55.
38 D. James Kennedy, Ph.D., p. 10.
39 *Handbook for Local Leaders*, National Education Association, 2007. http://www.nea.org/student-program/tools/handbook.html
40 "NEA: 2006 Handbook," National Education Association, 2006, p. 253. http://www.nea.org/handbook/images/handbookonline.pdf
41 Diana Jean Schemo, "Private Schools Perform Near Public Schools in Study," *The New York Times*, July 15, 2006. http://www.nytimes.com/2006/07/15/education/15report.html?ex=1310616000&en=abe9690ed35b306f&ei=5088&partner=rssnyt&emc=rss
42 David S. Hahn, "How Low Can We Go?," *The Wall Street Journal*, May 26, 2006. http://www.opinionjournal.com/taste/?id=110008433
43 Arthur Levine, "Educating School Leaders," Education Schools Project, March 2005. http://www.edschools.org/pdf/Final313.pdf
44 "Better Leaders for America's Schools: A Manifesto," The Thomas S. Fordham Institute, May 2003. http://www.broadfoundation.org/med-pubs/BetterLeadersforAmericasSchools.pdf
45 Ibid.
46 "Westminster Academy Statement of Faith," Westminster Academy, 2007. http://www.wacad.edu/general/statementoffaith.html#exist
47 Westminster Academy Mission Statement, 2007. http://westminster.novusedu.com/mission.html
48 "Westminster Academy 2004-2005 Annual Report," A Publication of Westminster Academy, 2005. http://www2.wacad.edu/pdf/annualreport04-05.pdf
49 "Florida's Average SAT Score Slips," St. Petersburg Times, August 31, 2005. http://www.sptimes.com/2005/08/31/State/Medicaid_pilot_projec.shtml
50 D. James Kennedy, Ph.D., p. 21.
51 D. James Kennedy, Ph.D., p. 25-26.

MORAL COLLAPSE

1 William J. Federer, *America's God and Country*, Amerisearch, Inc., St. Louis, Missouri, 2000.
2 David Barton, *Original Intent*, WallBuilder Press, Aledo, Texas, 2000, p. 153.
3 Karen MacPherson, "Study Finds Few Male, Minority Teachers," *Pittsburgh Post-Gazette*, August 28, 2003. http://www.post-gazette.com/pg/03240/215857.stm
4 "NEA: 2006 Handbook," National Education Association, 2006, p. 334. http://www.nea.org/handbook/images/handbookonline.pdf
5 *NEA: 2006 Handbook*, p. 290.
6 *NEA: 2006 Handbook*, p. 219-220.
7 *NEA: 2006 Handbook*, p. 294.
8 *NEA: 2006 Handbook*, p. 294.
9 "Finishing Up In Orlando," National Education Association, July 6, 2006. http://www.nea.org/annualmeeting/raaction/index.html
10 *NEA: 2006 Handbook*, p. 299.
11 *NEA: 2006 Handbook*, p. 294.
12 *NEA: 2006 Handbook*, p. 284.
13 "NEA-PAC and AFT-COPE Political Contributions Summary and Breakdown 1977 to March 25, 1998," The Education Policy Institute, 1998. http://www.educationpolicy.org/data-2.htm
14 George Archibald, "Pro-Life Teachers Angered by March, *The Washington Times*, April 19, 2004. http://www.washingtontimes.com/national/20040419-124027-8621r.htm
15 "Why You Should March," National Organization for Women, March 2004. http://march.now.org/whywemarch.html
16 *NEA: 2006 Handbook*, p. 97.
17 "PFAW Foundation: In the Courts," People for the American Way, 2007. http://www.pfaw.org/pfaw/general/default.aspx?oid=269
18 "Teachers' Pets," *The Wall Street Journal*, January 3, 2006. http://www.opinionjournal.com/editorial/feature.html?id=110007761
19 Amy Fagan, "Bush Seeks Teacher Merit-Pay Funds," *The Washington Times*, February 10, 2007. http://www.washtimes.com/national/20070210-115412-8424r.htm
20 "Education Chief's 'Terrorist' Remark Ignites Fury," *CNN News*, February 24, 2004. http://www.cnn.com/2004/EDUCATION/02/24/paige.terrorist.nea/
21 D. James Kennedy, Ph.D., *Education: Public Problems & Private Solutions*, Coral Ridge Ministries, Fort Lauderdale, FL, p. 24.

22 "NEA: 2006 Handbook," p. 44.

23 Chris Turner, "David Limbaugh: Discrimination Against Christians Surging," *Baptist Press*, January 12, 2004. http://www.bpnews.net/bpnews.asp?ID=17421

24 "Students Resources Page," GLSEN Website, 2007. http://www.glsen.org/cgi-bin/iowa/student/student/index.html

25 Dana Williams, "Gay-Straight Alliances: Here to Stay," Tolerance.org, May 23, 2003. http://www.tolerance.org/teens/stories/article.jsp?ar=48

26 Frank York, "Public Employees Teach Kids 'Gay' Sex," *WorldNetDaily*, May 9, 2000. http://www.wnd.com/news/article.asp?ARTICLE_ID=17490

27 Ibid.

28 "Fistgate Revisted," *Massachusetts News*, March 25, 2000. http://www.massnews.com/past_issues/other/8_Aug/auggs5.htm

29 "Students Fight Suspensions Over Handing Out Candy Canes," The Freedom Forum, January 3, 2003. http://www.freedomforum.org/templates/document.asp?documentID=17417

30 Joanna Weiss, "Explicit Pamphlets Displayed at School," *The Boston Globe*, May 19, 2005. http://www.boston.com/news/education/k_12/articles/2005/05/19/explicit_pamphlets_displayed_at_school/

31 Ethan Jacobs, "GLSEN-Gate Take Two," *The Bay Windows*, May 19, 2005. http://www.article8.org/docs/news_events/glsen_043005/conference.htm

32 EXTREMELY GRAPHIC: *The Little Black Book: Queer in the 21st Century*, Massachusetts AIDS Action Committee, 2005.

33 Ibid.

34 WHDH 7 News Report on Brookline High http://studio3d.com/download/PRC/WHDH%20black%20book%20may%2018%2005.wmv

35 "NEA Website Offers Resources on Anti-LGBT Bias and Behavior," GLSEN, December 19, 2006. http://www.glsen.org/cgi-bin/iowa/all/news/record/2021.html

36 "Dealing with Legal Matters Surrounding Students' Sexual Orientation and Gender Identity," The National Education Association, 2004, p. 9. http://www.nea.org/teachers/images/glbtguide.pdf

37 *Hansen v. Ann Arbor Public Schools*, No. 02-CV-72802-DT, U.S. District Judge Gerald E. Rosen, December 5, 2003. http://www.mied.uscourts.gov/_opinions/Rosenpdf/hansen.pdf

38 "School Censored Christian Student from Expressing Her Religious Views Against Homosexuality—Ordered to Pay $102,738," Thomas More Law Center, October 5, 2004. http://www.thomasmore.org/news.html?NewsID=238

39 *Hansen v. Ann Arbor Public Schools*. http://www.mied.uscourts.gov/_opinions/Rosenpdf/hansen.pdf

40 "N.Y.C. to Open High School for Gays," *FOX News*, July 28, 2003. http://www.foxnews.com/story/0,2933,93060,00.html

41 "First Public Gay High School to Open in NYC," *CNN News*, July 29, 2003. http://www.cnn.com/2003/EDUCATION/07/28/gay.school.ap/

42 Ibid.

43 "Homosexual Students 'Bust' Johns," *WorldNetDaily*, November 7, 2003. http://www.worldnetdaily.com/news/article.asp?ARTICLE_ID=35492

44 Max Jammer, *Einstein and Religion: Physics and Theology.* Princeton: Princeton University Press, 1999. http://www.quotationspage.com/quotes/Albert_Einstein/

45 "Nearly Two-thirds of U.S. Adults Believe Human Beings Were Created by God," Harris Poll, July 6, 2005. http://www.harrisinteractive.com/harris_poll/index.asp?PID=581

46 Joseph Maldonado, "Creation Debate Draws in Teachers," *The York Daily Record*, October 24, 2004. http://www.ydr.com/doverbiology/ci_3219354

47 "Dover Teachers Win Professional Ethics Battle," PSEA Voice Online, February 2005. http://www.psea.org/voice/article.cfm?artid=1586

48 "District Makes 'Intelligent Design' Statement Optional," The First Amendment Center, January 10, 2005. http://www.firstamendmentcenter.org/news.aspx?id=14664

49 *Kitzmiller v. Dover Area School District*, No. 04cv2688, U.S. District Court for the Middle District of Pennsylvania, December 20, 2005. http://www.pamd.uscourts.gov/kitzmiller/kitzmiller_342.pdf

50 Paula Reed Ward, "District in Evolution Debate to Pay $1 Million in Legal Fees," *The Pittsburgh Post-Gazette*, February 23, 2006. http://www.post-gazette.com/pg/06054/659758.stm

51 "Judge: Evolution Stickers Unconstitutional," CNN, January 14, 2005 http://www.cnn.com/2005/LAW/01/13/evolution.textbooks.ruling/

52 *Selman v. Cobb County*, Case No. 1 02-CV-2325-CC, January 13, 2005. http://www.aclu.org/FilesPDFs/cobb%20county%20decision.pdf

53 Ibid.

54 Dave Cullen, "Kill Mankind. No One Should Survive," Salon, September 23, 1999. http://www.salon.com/news/feature/1999/09/23/journal/print.html

55 "Stunning Documentary Links Darwin, Hitler," *WorldNetDaily*, February 12, 2007. http://www.worldnetdaily.com/news/article.asp?ARTICLE_ID=54218

56 *Fleming v. Jefferson County School District*, No. 01-1512, Tenth U.S. Circuit Court of Appeals, June 27, 2002. http://www.kscourts.org/ca10/cases/2002/06/01-1512.htm

57 "Judge Rules Islamic Education OK in California Classrooms," WorldNetDaily, December 13, 2003. http://www.worldnetdaily.com/news/article.asp?ARTICLE_ID=36118

58 "Judge OKs Islamic Role-Playing in Classroom," *San Francisco Chronicle*, December 12, 2003. http://www.sfgate.com/cgi-bin/article.cgi?file=/c/a/2003/12/12/MNGBN3L90R10.DTL

59 Ibid.

60 "Judge Rules Islamic Education OK in California Classrooms," WorldNetDaily, December 13, 2003. http://www.worldnetdaily.com/news/article.asp?ARTICLE_ID=36118

61 Doug Powers, "Schoolhouse Crock: Sexual Eminent Domain," *WorldNetDaily*, November 7, 2005. http://www.worldnetdaily.com/news/article.asp?ARTICLE_ID=47267

62 "Oral Sex Hot Topic at School Board," *WorldNetDaily*, January 26, 2006. http://www.worldnetdaily.com/news/article.asp?ARTICLE_ID=48507

63 "Parents Sue to Block 'Pro-Gay' Classes," *WorldNetDaily*, May 3, 2005. http://www.worldnetdaily.com/news/article.asp?ARTICLE_ID=44099

64 "Cucumber-Condom Video Online," *WorldNetDaily*, March 11, 2005. http://www.worldnetdaily.com/news/article.asp?ARTICLE_ID=43238

65 George Archibald, "'How To Be Gay' Course Draws Fire at Michigan," *The Washington Times*, August 18, 2003. http://www.washingtontimes.com/national/20030818-122317-3268r.htm

66 "U.S. Department of Education, Office of the Under Secretary, *Educator Sexual Misconduct: A Synthesis of Existing Literature*, Washington, D.C., 2004. http://www.ed.gov/rschstat/research/pubs/misconductreview/report.pdf

67 Ibid., p. 17.

68 Ibid., p. 18.

69 Ibid., p. 44.

70 Neal McCluskey, "Why We Fight: How Public Schools Cause Social Conflict," Executive Summary, The Cato Institute, January 2007.

PARENTS VS. THE STATE

1 James V. Wertsch, *Voices of Collective Remembering*, Cambridge University Press, 2002.

2 *Pierce v. Society of the Sisters of the Holy Names of Jesus and Mary*, 268 U.S. 510, Supreme Court of the United States, June 1, 1925. http://caselaw.lp.findlaw.com/cgi-bin/getcase.pl?court=us&vol=268&invol=510

3 The OYEZ Project, Pierce v. Society of Sisters, 268 U.S. 510 (1925). http://www.oyez.org/cases/case?case=1901-1939/1924/1924_583

4 *Pierce v. Society of the Sisters*

5 Adolf Hiter, "Party Program of the NSDAP," Yale University Avalon Project, February 24, 1920.

6 " 'Homeschooling Illegal' Declares German School Official," Home School Legal Defense Association, January 7, 2005. http://www.hslda.org/hs/international/Germany/200501100.asp

7 Bob Unruh, "Achtung! Germany Drags Homeschool Kids to Class," *WorldNetDaily*, October 25, 2006.

8 "Parental Choice: Homeschooling or Jail?," The Home School Court Report, Volume XXI, Number 3, June 2005. http://www.hslda.org/courtreport/V21N3/V21N308.asp

9 *Fritz Konrad v. Germany*, Application No. 35504/03, European Court of Human Rights, September 11, 2006.

10 Bob Egelko, "Suit Over Sex Questions Reaches Supreme Court," *The San Francisco Chronicle*, August 30, 2006. http://www.sfgate.com/cgi-bin/article.cgi?f=/c/a/2006/08/30/BAGM7KRQFD1.DTL

11 *Fields v. Palmdale School District*, No. 03-56499, Ninth U.S. Circuit Court of Appeals, November 2, 2005. http://www.ca9.uscourts.gov/ca9/newopinions.nsf/E8695945B7C6F6B5882570AD0051320A/$file/0356499.pdf?openelement

12 Ibid.

13 Supreme Court Turns Down Parents Who Complained about Student Sex Survey," *San Diego Union-Tribune*, December 4, 2006. http://www.signonsandiego.com/news/education/20061204-0728-scotus-sexsurvey.html

14 "Don't Say They're Wrong," ADF Press Release, February 15, 2005. http://www.alliancedefensefund.org/news/story.aspx?cid=3338

15 "Ky. Students Can't Skip Anti-Gay Harassment Training," First Amendment Center, February 20, 2006. http://www.firstamendmentcenter.org/news.aspx?id=16508

16 "View Homosexual Film or School Faces Lawsuit," *WorldNetDaily*, November 28, 2004. http://www.worldnetdaily.com/news/article.asp?ARTICLE_ID=41667

17 *Tinker v. Des Moines Independent Community School District*, 393 U.S. 503, Supreme Court of the United States, February 24, 1969. http://caselaw.lp.findlaw.com/scripts/getcase.pl?court=

US&vol=393&invol=503
18 *Parker v. Hurley*, U.S. District Court for the District of Massachusetts, April 27, 2006. http://www.massresistance.org/docs/parker_lawsuit/complaint.html
19 Bob Unruh, "Judge Orders 'Gay' Agenda Taught to Christian Children," *WorldNetDaily*, February 24, 2007. http://www.worldnetdaily.com/news/article.asp?ARTICLE_ID=54420
20 *Parker v. Hurley*.
21 *Parker v. Hurley*, Civil Action No. 06-1 075 1 MLW, Defendants' Motion to Dismiss, October 16, 2006. http://www.massresistance.org/docs/parker_lawsuit/defendants_reply.pdf
22 *Parker v. Town of Lexington*, Civil Action No. 06-CV-10751-MLW, Amicus Brief, September 20, 2006. http://www.massresistance.org/docs/parker_lawsuit/aclu_brief.pdf
23 *Parker v. Town of Lexington*, No. 06-CV-10751-MLW, U. S. District Judge Mark L. Wolf, February 23, 2007. http://www.massresistance.org/docs/parker_lawsuit/order_motion_to_dismiss_022307.pdf
24 Milton Friedman, "Public Schools: Make Them Private," The Cato Institute, June 23, 1995. http://www.cato.org/pubs/briefs/bp-023.html
25 Martin Kasindorf, "Christian School Suing UC Over College Credits," *USA Today*, January 12, 2006. http://www.usatoday.com/news/nation/2006-01-12-christian-school_x.htm
26 Mike Weiss, "Culture War Pits UC vs. Christian Way of Teaching," *The San Francisco Chronicle*, December 12, 2005.
27 University of California 2005-2006 Annual Report, Audited Statements, June 30, 2006. http://www.universityofcalifornia.edu/annualreport/2006/pdf/auditedstatements.pdf
28 Lynn Vincent, "Strange Standards," *WORLD Magazine*, Vol. 20, No. 46, November 26, 2005. http://www.worldmag.com/articles/11299
29 Mike Weiss.
30 "Federal Budget: Receipts and Outlays," American Presidency Project, University of California, Santa Barbara, 2005. http://www.presidency.ucsb.edu/data/budget.php
31 "10 Facts About K-12 Education Funding," U.S. Department of Education, June 2005. http://www.ed.gov/about/overview/fed/10facts/10facts.pdf
32 "Joint Statement of Henry Paulson, Secretary of the Treasury, and Robert Portman, Director of the Office of Management and Budget, on Budget Results for Fiscal Year 2006," U.S. Department of the Treasury, October 12, 2006. http://www.ustreas.gov/press/releases/hp135.htm
33 "Bernanke: Baby Boomers Threaten Economy," *CNN Money*, January 18, 2007. http://money.cnn.com/2007/01/18/news/economy/bernanke.reut/index.htm?postversion=2007011815

ALTERNATIVES THAT WORK

1 President Ronald Reagan, Radio Address to the Nation on Education, *Public Papers of Ronald Reagan*, p. 622.
2 Richard Sousa and Hanna Skandera, "Learning at Home," The Hoover Institution, 2003. http://www.hoover.org/publications/digest/3057621.html
3 "Trends in Private School Enrollments," National Center for Education Statistics, 2006. http://nces.ed.gov/programs/coe/2006/section1/indicator04.asp
4 Caroline M. Hoxby, "Achievement in Charter Schools and Regular Public Schools in the United States: Understanding the Differences," Harvard University and National Bureau of Economic Research, December 2004. http://www.economics.harvard.edu/faculty/hoxby/papers/hoxbycharter_dec.pdf
5 Rob Reich, *Bridging Liberalism and Multiculturalism in American Education,*University of Chicago Press, 2002. http://www.ksg.harvard.edu/m-rcbg/youngfaculty/papers/Homeschooling2002.pdf
6 Lawrence M. Rudner, "The Scholastic Achievement of Home School Students," Education Resources Information Center Clearinghouse on Assessment and Evaluation, September 1999.
7 Ibid.
8 "Classical Christian Education," *Wikipedia*, November 29, 2006. http://en.wikipedia.org/wiki/Classical_Christian_education
9 *Digest of Education Statistics,* (NCES 2006-030), Chapter 1, 2005. http://nces.ed.gov/fastfacts/display.asp?id=65
10 Stephen P. Broughman and Kathleen W. Pugh, "Characteristics of Private Schools in the United States: Results from the 2001-2002 Private School Universe Survey," *Education Statistics Quarterly*, Volume 6, Issue 4. http://nces.ed.gov/programs/quarterly/vol_6/6_4/4_2.asp
11 "Student Achievement in Private Schools," National Assessment of Educational Progress, U.S. Department of Education, 2005, Executive Summary. http://nces.ed.gov/nationsreportcard/pdf/studies/2006459.pdf
12 Ibid., p. 7. http://nces.ed.gov/nationsreportcard/pdf/studies/2006459.pdf
13 Dan Lips and Evan Feinberg, "School Choice: 2006 Progress Report," The Heritage Foundation, September 18, 2006. http://www.heritage.org/Research/Education/upload/bg_1970.pdf
14 Teresa Mendez, "Can Competition Really Improve Schools," *Christian Science Monitor*,

September 7, 2004. http://www.csmonitor.com/2004/0907/p12s01-legn.html
15 Dan Lips and Evan Feinberg.
16 Dan Lips and Evan Feinberg.
17 Marshall Fritz, "Bad News for Freedom-Lovers," Alliance for the Separation of School and State, July 19, 2002. http://www.honestedu.org/essays/fritz/bad_news.php
18 Paul E. Peterson, William G. Howell, and Jay P. Greene, "An Evaluation of the Cleveland Voucher Program After Two Years," John F. Kennedy School of Government, Harvard University, June 1999. http://www.ksg.harvard.edu/pepg/PDF/Papers/clev2ex.pdf
19 Ibid.
20 D. James Kennedy, Ph.D., *Education: Public Problems & Private Solutions*, Coral Ridge Ministries, Fort Lauderdale, FL, p. 56.
21 *Zelman v. Simmons-Harris*, No. 00-1751, Supreme Court of the United States, June 27, 2002. http://supct.law.cornell.edu/supct/pdf/00-1751P.ZO
22 Dan Lips and Evan Feinberg.
23 Lisa Graham Keegan, "Tuition Tax Credits: A Model for School Choice," National Center for Policy Analysis, December 12, 2001. http://www.ncpa.org/pub/ba/ba384/
24 "Just the FAQs—Tuition Tax Credits and Tax Deductions," Center for Education Reform, 2007. http://www.edreform.com/index.cfm?fuseAction=document&documentID=59§ionID=67
25 David Salisbury, "Are Education Tax Credits on the Way?," The Cato Institute, June 22, 2002. http://www.cato.org/dailys/06-22-02.html
26 Dr. Albert Mohler, "Needed: An Exit Strategy," Albert Mohler Commentary, June 17, 2005. http://www.albertmohler.com/commentary_read.php?cdate=2005-06-17
27 Jim Brown and Allie Martin, "Presbyterians, Baptists Concerned About Public Schools' Worldly Influence on Children," *Agape Press*, June 16, 2005 http://headlines.agapepress.org/archive/6/162005a.asp
28 Ibid.
29 Dr. Albert Mohler.
30 President Ronald Reagan, Radio Address to the Nation on Education, *Public Papers of Ronald Reagan*, p. 622.